MW01228863

DIVINE DIALOGUE

INSIGHTS FROM GOD,
THE VIRGIN MARY & BEYOND

JOELLE C BURNS

© Joelle Burns

This is dedicated to my family and friends.

Thank you all for the support and love on this journey we call life.

PROLOGUE

This story came to me through the knowledge that I have been given and shown through God and the Divine. I am a divine medium, which means I connect, but am not limited to, God and the Divine. This includes all the information I have been shown through God and also my personal experiences and journey. I am a person, just like you. I was raised in the Catholic faith and went to church; I still attend church. This book isn't about changing who you are but about understanding who you are on a soul level. Who you were brought to be on this earth.

I believe you all have the ability to connect with God and the Divine. Sometimes, we just need to quiet our minds and listen. When I connect and speak with the Divine or God, I always say they talk in riddles and loop the same sentence to me over and over again. This is because they don't want to intervene on our free will but gently guide us along our way in life.

As you will read on, the first section of the book is where I connect with God. In the middle are conversations with the Virgin Mary, and at the end are the conversations I have had most recently with an alien named Adam.

I hope you enjoy it!

CHAPTER 1

GOD

"For in me, I see you

For in you, I see me."

-God

I said out loud, "Ok God, I'm listening."

God answered,
"You have always been listening, my child."

That was my first shocking communication with God.

You see, I haven't always had this gift of being a psychic medium or being able to communicate with God and the divine. I had what you would call a normal upbringing in a quiet town in upstate New York. My family was not wealthy or poor, and we lived comfortably, as my mother would like to say. Our family didn't have much, but we loved and laughed often. On Sundays, we frequently visited the Catholic Church in the town over from us. If me and my siblings behaved at church, we would go to a little cafe on the corner, which is just a couple of blocks away from the church. You could get the best New York-style coffee cake that you have ever experienced. It was always a real treat, and I tried to behave and sit still through church as a little girl. I still attend church to this day, but I have always found that I don't really fit the mold of what a churchgoer should be or look like. Be proper, sit quietly, obey all the rules, and follow all the guidelines, and God won't send you straight to Hell. I was sure I didn't follow all of the rules, so was I damned and going straight to Hell? Yikes, what a way to live. I never really challenged the church; I just sometimes felt out of place, you know what I mean?

As a little girl, I was always the sensitive one, off crying in a corner or being picked on by my siblings. To be honest, I did cry a lot. Now, looking back and understanding that I was an empath and just sensitive nature, having more insight and intuition than others really set the foundation for my current reality. I have always been an empath, and I was told by multiple mediums that I had this ability, and I would answer, "Yup, uh huh," without fully grasping what it actually meant. An empath is a person who is highly sensitive to other people's feelings or emotions. If someone walks by an empath and is angry, it can switch our emotions on a dime.

The main levels of an empath are emotional, physical, and intuitive. Some people will experience one, or someone like myself will experience all three. Understanding that you are an empath can help you navigate life more easily. This sensitivity can make it very difficult for an empath to be in large crowds or work under pressure around others. I have realized that if I could go back in time and tell my high school self, listen, you need to go test in a room by yourself, where you can't feel others' anxiety around you. You will test so much better. Man, I wish I knew this growing up. Instead of being a semi-B student, I would have probably had all A's.

When I graduated high school, I went straight into the field that I still currently work in as a massage therapist. As a highly sensitive empath, when working with clients, I would physically feel and take their pain from their bodies into my own. For example, many times, I would be massaging someone's back, and I would physically feel my right knee hurt. And I usually wouldn't want to interrupt the quiet of the massage session, so I would push it away. But the pain would persist, and then the feeling of anxiety would hit me (which I now understand was a spirit trying to guide me). So, at that point, between the pain and the anxiety, I felt compelled to ask my client, "Do you have any pain in your right knee?" And nine times out of ten, they would answer, "Yes, I have had an issue there for a while," or something of that nature. This would also be an ailment that we did not previously discuss or have written down in their client intake form before the session.

Most of you, actually, let me rephrase that all of you have the ability to be an empath and psychic medium abilities as well. There is nothing about me that is so completely different from you. Everyone can do what I do; it's just if you can quiet your mind enough to allow any thoughts, emotions, for spirit to come in. This is where society gets so consumed by everything around us that we don't take the time to listen. Even I, as a busy mom of two small boys, find it very difficult to find a quiet space. And to even quiet my mind to allow communication from spirit to come in.

I have not been a psychic medium for all that long. About a year ago, I got hit by what I call psychic lightning. It just freakin' hit me one day. It was crazy. I'll further explain: I was having a conversation with my cousin over the phone, and we were discussing her daughter, who was coming into her mediumship abilities. We talked about her taking some classes, expanding her consciousness, and entering that spiritual enlightenment. I was really amazed by learning about her gifts and her abilities. I remember feeling elated as we were talking about her experiences and thinking, "That is so cool." So, we ended our conversation, and I remember just going about my day but really thinking about my little cousin with her medium gifts and capabilities. I remember picturing where she was in the world and what she was doing, picturing what her day looked like. I have always been imaginative, and it has always come easy to me if someone would say picture a "white boat on a stormy day with a red sail." I could see that boat as clear as day by using my third eye or my intuition. Your third eye is located on your forehead between your eyebrows and slightly above. This is also what mediums call our area of clairvoyance. Clairvoyance is the perception of seeing something that is not physically in front of you. This is often a medium's way to connect with spirit.

So, as I was going about my day and thinking of my little cousin. I activated my third eye without even knowing it. This is also what is called "tuning in "to someone's energy. Tuning in is exactly what I was doing, which was thinking of that one person.

Picturing and knowing where they are in space and time. What state are they in, in the US? What does it look like around this particular person? Is it cloudy or sunny? What are they wearing? How are they feeling? This is not something I do often now as a medium because it feels a little like invading someone's privacy. But I did do it often before I became a medium for any friends or family, I think just out of curiosity.

After I had done this exercise of "tuning into" my cousin, I believe I noticed the next day that I physically had changes going on in my body. The lower part of the back of my head, the anatomical location, would be the occipital lobe of the brain; that whole area felt like it was tingling, itching, and vibrating. This went on nonstop for about a week or so. I was massaging a client at the end of the week, and this phenomenon was happening to me. When I work with my massage clients, I am usually in a very calm, almost meditative state. The vibrating was happening so badly while I was working on this client one day that I was physically tapping or hitting it to make it go away. Guess what? It still persisted.

So, I asked myself, "What is going on? "

And I heard an answer, "*Spirit is trying to communicate with you*".

This is all happening while I am still actively working on my client. Thank goodness I have been in the massage business for over 20 years, and I can practically do it blindfolded.

I thought to myself, did I just hear an answer that wasn't my own? I was totally confused about what was happening to me. Mind you, I heard that answer, "*Spirit is trying to communicate with you*," in my own mind's voice. So, I thought to myself, well am I going crazy? What is happening?

I don't believe I did much else that day to ask questions or delve deeper into the unknown knowledge that I had just received.

I remember having to work the next day with clients, and in the massages, the vibrating intensified. So, I remember thinking, ok, well, if the spirit is trying to communicate with me, what do they want to say? So, I was working on a female client who was there with her husband for a couple's massage. This is what I heard:

"*My name is Rose.*" "*Ask her about the new sports car she got.*" She said, "*I think it's a Mustang, but I'm not good with cars. It's red, really sharp-looking.*"

I did not know who Rose was, but I intuitively knew there was a relationship between Rose and this female client that I was working on. I continued the massage without saying a word, but I battled internally about whether I should mention something to my client. I decided not to say anything. I figured the client came in to get a massage, not a message from their deceased loved one. So, I held my tongue. I went about my day with other clients and am still pondering over the messages that I had received. As I finished up and said my goodbyes to my coworkers, I headed out the back entrance of the spa. The rear entrance of the spa has a small parking lot for our clients, maybe a whole of 6 parking spaces. And we, as employees, parked in a separate parking lot. I have worked at this spa multiple times, and every time I exit, the cars in the parking lot are usually black or white SUVs or cars, nothing really flashy. Well, to my surprise, as I was leaving work that day, guess what was out there? A red Mustang or sports car. I'm not good with cars either. At that point, I received full body chills all over (which I now know is confirmation from spirit and my spirit guides) as I thought to myself, "Holy Shit" maybe I was connecting and communicating with someone in that massage.

When I came home, I was really excited to tell my husband what had just happened to me. My husband is so very sweet, and I love him so, but his cynical side came out, and he answered, "Oh, ya? If you are communicating with spirit, why don't you read me?" I said "OK". So, there I was having no idea what I was doing, but I shut my eyes quieted down and just heard, felt, and sensed spirit with me. And then I began channeling. I was able to communicate with his past grandparents, whom I had never even met. I was able to tell him what they looked like and how they dressed and get a sense of their personalities. I understood and knew a lot of things that spirit had shown me in that moment that I never knew about his family.

It was all pretty amazing and still surreal, but instead of running away from this gift I felt the need to lean into it and embrace it. I was sure people were going to pass judgment on me and think I was crazy. But for the first time, it felt like I was living my dream life of who I had always known I could be.

As time passed, I learned to harness my abilities, and I am deeply grateful for the opportunity to share messages of love and comfort with those who need them most. I understand that many people don't fully comprehend what I do, and I know that the unknown can be intimidating. But that's alright. I'm not here to prove my worth or my abilities to anyone. What I hope people come to understand is that mediums aren't mystical or dangerous beings in a trance, practicing something dark or sinister. Instead, I'm simply a vessel. My soul steps into the astral plane, connects with your loved ones, and acts as a bridge for a conversation between you and them. In those brief, beautiful moments, you are reunited. There is nothing evil or satanic about it—if anything, it makes me feel even closer to God.

Which gets me back on the topic of how I started communicating with God. As I was still learning and growing my gift, I would often feel the tingling sensation on my head where I would have the knowing that spirit was trying to communicate with me. This one time after running around with the kids, carpool lines and mountains of laundry to do, and finishing cleaning up from dinner when I was finally sitting down for the evening after trying to relax after a long day at work.

I felt a big vibration on the right side of my head. Now, when I normally feel a vibration or spirit, it can be small or feel very centrally located, almost like a pinpoint area. But this particular day, I felt my entire right side of my head go bonkers. And when I feel vibration come in (if I'm not too tired, that is) I quiet down and focus on who may be wanting to get my attention.

Guess what I heard? Abraham. I said, "OK." But I wasn't sure who Abraham was just yet. But since I felt this vibration/tingling in such a big area of my head, I knew it was someone of great importance. Now, some of you reading this may be very fluent in the Bible or Biblical texts. I, however, am not. As I have mentioned before, I did go to church growing up, but did I pay any attention? No.

So, I continued to ask Abraham, "Aren't you an angel?" Abraham answered,

"Yes. We are in the same family, and you came here to Earth to help teach the people."

I asked, "Teach them about what?".

Abraham answered, *"Teach them about love."*

I must be going crazy, I thought to myself. What the heck is going on here? I am completely new to my gifts of being a medium, and now I am having conversations with biblical persons. I was scared to even speak to my husband, who was supportive yet skeptical about me being a medium. Feeling overwhelmed and not worthy, I thought, why me? The next day, I wrote down that Abraham made me feel I was supposed to create a space for people to learn, teach, grow, and heal. I had no idea what this meant or how this would come to fruition. Even as I am writing this book to you all, having pen to paper, I am still not sure of what exactly Abraham was speaking of. But I know that Abraham has asked me to write down the truth of God.

Chapter 2

What am I to write?

The truth of God.

But hasn't that been written before?

Yes, in many texts and languages across the world and galaxies. I am the one true source that ties everything in the cosmos together. I am the centripetal force, as you will, of creation. The catalyst to all life. I have you writing this book because people need hope. And with hope, they have love, which is how we help and heal what is broken worldwide. To give life is my greatest accomplishment. I don't discern any differences between beings from different planets. You are a part of me, as they are a part of God. Can't you see me all around you? I am the first flower in the springtime or the first look into your child's eyes.

Love is sometimes lost in the world, and I want to speak through you to help people reconnect with who they truly are.

And who is that?

They are truly of me. When a child is born, it is from the perfect biological genetics of both mother and father. This is the same as with God. I am creator of all, and hence I am creator of people, and I am within every soul.

You just previously stated, 'I don't discern any differences between beings from different planets'. Are you talking about extraterrestrials?

Of course. There is nothing in all the universes I have not created, including what you (as humans) call extraterrestrial. There is no limitation to the expansion and creation of my universes, including the beings who inhabit them. This includes different galactic beings that have multiple differences that are specific to each being and their planets. But there is nothing more equitable and fragile than human beings. I created the earth as a beautiful, self-sustaining ecosystem of elaborate, harmonious balances. Humans have created an imbalance in the ecosystem with industrialized revolutions and modern technologies. This balance can be restored through ridding the world of outdated cultural systems that impede the environment. The human race has evolved to comply with these new theologies to help the earth heal from global warming, air pollution, pollution of the oceans, and so on.

Some call this new evolution the New Earth. This has been discussed in spiritual circles across the world. The New Earth is not a physical secondary Earth; it is a renewed and reborn Earth you live on now. As the human race is growing and evolving, it will grow into a super sensitive supreme being that has all the enlightenment of the balance of the universe and everything living in it. This place will not require nutrition from meat; it will be more of a vegetarian diet if any diet is needed. It depends on their level of evolution. Humans will be taller than they are now, and all will have similar, small-frame builds. These awakened people of Earth will have a full understanding of the Yin and Yang, or the give and take of how the universe works. Enlightened beings will not just pick a flower that is growing along their walking path; they will most likely choose not to pick it, just to bring it home and admire it until it dies. But to enjoy its beauty where it stays if it is not necessary for nutritional or medicinal use.

You see, I created everything in nature to be able to help humans, from scratch on their knees to cancer or even dementia. These enlightened humans will not necessarily need as much medicinal use because they will have the knowledge of pure nutrition, lotions, and supplements that will keep their bodies functioning at optimal health.

So, when you say awakened or enlightened humans, does it mean the same thing? And how far are we from this so-called New Earth? How do we evolve and get ourselves there?

You are beginning to understand and get excited about my teachings and speaking with you. I like this side of you. Ok, let's talk about enlightened humans; what does that mean? For one to become enlightened, one will have already gone through the awakening stage. To become awakened is the initial onset of coming into the knowledge of all-knowing and understanding the universe as I have created it.

This change can happen very slowly for some, or like you, they will have a rapid awakening and be like a baby bird for a little while. Not exactly sure of how to get to their feet. In an awakened state, your conscious being does not make decisions out of any extreme emotion. When your soul evolves into a more enlightened state, this is the experience that you can present in the current time of fully understanding dualities and the consciousness of love, the universe, and all things.

The New Earth is happening now. The shift has been set in motion. It is said this shift of New Earth started in 2012, but it started from the Earth's core and went back to the 1960s. It is all about the earth changing and shifting into a new positive vibration and the people of Earth following suit. All will eventually evolve into this enlightened state, but it all starts with shifting your consciousness and living more positively.

How do we get to this state?

This is a process all souls must find on their own. What will be an answer for one person to become enlightened may not be the same for the next. But the root of all things of evolution is to do everything with love. And this is not a fake throwing someone a bone just because God told you to send love. This is where you feel it in your soul to understand, free yourself of, and release any negative emotions towards a person, place, or thing. You will need to use less judgment on others.

Yes, I understand this is not easy for everyone, but it is where your soul is meant to go in enlightenment. Many human beings have achieved full enlightenment, and one of them was Gandhi. Gandhi achieved this by actively practicing no judgment on another person, place, or thing. Ghandi sat in silence to better understand me, him, and the universe. He listened for answers within himself to help humanity. Through his selfless acts, he was able to achieve enlightenment. It was not an easy road for him. Many of his colleagues passed doubt or fear of his new ways of doing and teaching. It was a little too forward-thinking for some. But where do all the great teachings come from in the world? Does it come from those who do the same thing as everyone else is doing? Or do they step out of the box and not follow the societal norm? They are usually called names: crazy, out of touch with reality...

Change would never happen if there were no creative thinkers and expansive minds. I implore you (people of the world) to challenge life in the way it was meant to be challenged, going against the grain and following your heart with love and God in your corner. You are ready for the fight. One of my biggest lessons in life is how to find and keep faith in God.

Share your story of your meditation.

16

The one I experienced today?

Yes.

I'm not sure people will believe me.

It is not meant for the people who don't believe; it is meant for a message of hope. I know you're scared, but go ahead. Have Faith.

Ok. I will write it as I wrote in my journal just this morning. I recently had to go to the emergency room; I was experiencing paresthesia (full-body numbness). I also have been feeling off emotionally lately. I am usually a happy, upbeat person. I have been feeling anxious and not fully connected. I feel just off, and it sucks. It could be stress related, as my husband is taking on a new job. We almost had to move to Florida.

So, I did an anxiety release meditation, which was a guided meditation. Instead of fully listening to the meditation, my spirit guides said to me, "*You are going to be OK, and you need this (the meditation).*"

I asked if I could lay with God to feel God's love, and Jesus was there, and I released the anxiety. I was being washed with God's loving golden light all through my body. I started feeling a little sad, and as I did, Jesus came and cradled me just like a baby. And then I physically wept. I cried big tears. And Jesus said,

"*You see, this is how I keep you in tough times. You must keep the faith and know that I am carrying you through your toughest times. I am here for you always.*"

Jesus made me feel that this is how he looks after us all. I wept until I felt safe. I nuzzled my face in Jesus's neck and took a deep breath in.

It was so beautiful and so powerful. I thanked my spirit guides, Jesus, and God.

I came out of that meditation feeling much lighter, and I felt my faith renewed. Sometimes, we need a reset. What a beautiful message from Jesus.

What else would you like me to say?

Let's start at the beginning, which is; what happens when a person dies? This is one of the biggest and most controversial questions on earth. The body is not of anything other than matter here on earth. We must understand the soul to understand what happens when a person dies. The soul is a vibrational entity that is made of God. I created you, so why can't you be God's source? I have the highest frequency of vibrational beings. So, you see, you are a soul living in a chamber of earthly matter. You move in linear time and space when you are physically in your body; Earth is a three-dimensional reality. When there are infinite dimensions across different galaxies. I share this context with you in the most primitive form due to the limitation of language. Speech can hold me back from fully explaining the worldly dynamics that such is life.

The soul comes into reality when it is formed from a part of my Source energy. It is almost like having an atom, which splits off into another atom. They are completely identical and do not have any less energy than the other; they are equal. This is how all beings from different galaxies are the same because they are all equally a part of me, God.

This spark of who you truly are can be forgotten when living a life here on earth. There are too many distractions; life gets in the way. I want you to always connect with me and listen because I am always talk with you. This never has a hold on who we are as human beings.

Do you know that no energy can't connect with me? I designed you all that way. I want you to understand who I am. I am the alpha and omega; all things seen and unseen. There is nothing before me, and there will be nothing after me. I want you all to understand how powerful you are. Your thoughts and prayers are heard, and I will never leave your side in times of need.

Can't you see that you have everything you want at your fingertips? All you have to do is focus all your thoughts and energy, and you can get that dream car or the love of your life. There is nothing holding you back but yourself.

But I don't know if that is always true. What about people who have limitations, either financially or physically? Let's face it I haven't always been rolling in the dough here.

Tell me, where has your mindset been? Have you been focused on rolling in the dough, as you say, or have you been problem-solving and juggling multiple jobs and multiple tasks all at once? Here's how it works: don't just think, I want to be rich or roll in the dough. You have to take what it means to be rich and picture what that lifestyle will look like for you. You can picture it, can't you? Feel the textures of the clothes you would like to buy, and hold the keys to the fancy, expensive car you want to drive. This is the limitless manifestation that every human has and is very well capable of. As I have mentioned before, you are all powerful beings, and these powers go beyond your comprehension.

Material things do not mean anything to me. But I understand it can be of great importance for the people of earth. I want you to try a 2-week experiment. Let's start with something small. Let's have you manifest free ice cream, for starters. Ok, so first, I want you to picture the type of ice cream. What are you holding in your hand? Does it have sprinkles? Is it in a cup or a cone? What does the ice cream place look like? Are you inside or outside? Whom might you be enjoying this ice cream with? And when you receive a gift of free ice cream, how did it make you feel?

This is a small way of showing you how you can align anything in your path by choice. You have the power, and I want you to understand just how special and powerful you are.

So, as you see, there are no real financial limitations; there may be setbacks at certain times. **But greatness does not come from succeeding without failure.**

As for people who have physical limitations. There are ways for them to help manifest themselves well. For example, some people have experienced a false diagnosis of cancer, let's say. After the person receives this diagnosis (they don't yet know it's a false diagnosis), they start to feel lethargic and unwell. Their minds will start collecting the negative energy attached to such news. This will, then, truly make them sick. It may not make them come down immediately with cancer, but if it was a misdiagnosis that went on for years, then there is a possibility of that. See how your thoughts and mind can control the environment around you.

Some of the most successful people will go to a signing agreement deal that, in their mind, is already signed and completed. They will imagine shaking hands with the CEO and how they will feel on completion. It is this confidence —not cocky, but the confidence of knowing. That is the manifestation or manipulation of the universe.

Did you say cocky? And Manipulation?

Yes. Who do you believe created that emotion? I am the creator of everything.

CHAPTER 3

"Speak the truth and know." -Abraham

God has always been in existence. God is the energy of all things, and everything is made from God; matter, water, an atom, the atmosphere, the earth, humans, other planets, other galactic beings, other galaxies, other universes, etc. God is the creator. There was never a time before God. God exceeds all time, space, and energy.

God is made of perfect energy and that energy cannot be created or destroyed.

When I go into a meditation to sit and be in God's presence, an overwhelming sense of love washes over me.

One day, after sitting in meditation with my spirit guides, I wrote down this experience: "How am I supposed to use my gift?" They said I am to use everything I have been taught to help the mental and physical well-being of others. As my body lay still in meditation, in my mind's eye, my highest spirit guide, Abid, wanted to take me to sit with God.

Abid first appeared to me as a dark blueish amoeba-looking thing. He was all sparkly and never had any real shape; he just sort of looked like a fluid-standing sphere.

He told me he had never been here on earth and was just comfortable showing me himself in his natural form. When I asked him to look human, he now comes to me as a tall Indian-looking man.

As Abid took my hand, I felt this pull in an upward motion, and my body lay still in meditation. Then we came to a stop, and I realized I was now in the presence of God. God looks like the warmest, most illuminating light that flows through and around everything. It's almost like the sun, but without burning your eyes and having this overwhelming feeling of love emanating from its core. As I looked around, I saw that soft, pillowy clouds were over everything. The clouds reflected a glowing gold color coming from the presence of God, who was at the center of everything. As I looked around, I noticed other people and beings were there with me, along with my guide, Abid. I lay down on what seemed to be a cloud and just enjoyed and relaxed in the presence of God.

As I lay there soaking up the love from God, feeling like the warm sun on my skin. God came down and appeared to me in human form, almost like Jesus. As he stood before me, he looked so beautiful, and slowly and gently, he walked towards me, bent over, and kissed me on my forehead, where my third eye is. The third eye is linked to intuition through an activated pineal gland that is connected to all consciousness and knowing. I was physically crying at this point in my meditation. It was so profound, and I saw God go around and do the same to the other people and beings on these clouds. I came down and slowly awoke from meditation; I wiped the tears from my eyes and could barely lift my head because it felt so heavy and throbbing from the kiss.

I was so overwhelmed after this meditation; it has been months since this meditation experience until I am writing this book now. I didn't feel worthy enough to actually connect with God and, soon to find out, connect to the Divine. I am not the chosen one, nor am I acting in any way of that nature. Since becoming a medium connecting with people who have passed over for clients, family, and friends. I have understood more of the purpose of everything in the universe and alignment for all.

God, the creator, made man to have human experiences; there is free will for every human being.

Free will is the power of humans to make decisions or perform actions independently of any prior event or state of the universe. God is within all things on this Earth, living and nonliving, good or bad. We are all vibrational beings, and our vibration originates from the one true source, God.

Emanating from our soul is its own specific vibrational frequency, which gives off light and heat that is not detected by the naked eye. It is located near our diaphragm, where our soul resides within us. This is the true essence of who we all are and where we come from. Metaphysically speaking, it is how we are connected to other beings, of earth or not of this earth, and it's how we are connected to God.

God made other galactic beings from different galaxies and universes. There are many types of intergalactic beings. I have had personal encounters and experiences. I understand that God not only made man, but God made many beings on different planets. Some of my alien encounters have mostly involved seeing UFOs (unidentified flying objects) or UAPs (unidentified anomalous phenomena). I have shared my experiences with different newspapers and podcasts. These experiences have made me contemplate the vastness of our universe and all the wonders that we have yet to discover. Speaking with God and the divine has shown me that humans are not the only beings in our universe or other universes.

I do believe that I notice and receive alien activity due to my psychic sensitivities. I believe that aliens will regulate how we evolve and move into a more enlightened state. An enlightened person has a better grasp on the perception of reality and is not focused on what is happening to or around them in society.

We forget this before coming to earth because we agree to a mental cleanse before we reincarnate.

Reincarnation is when a soul returns to earth after a life has lived and died here. Earth is one of the hardest planets to be on to help educate and move our souls into a rapid acceleration of lifting our vibration, soul and energy.

Every single one of us has the same purpose as a soul: to elevate our vibration to be closer to God. God is the highest vibration or light source there is. We ascend to get closer to God.

I asked God, "What is the truth I am supposed to tell"?

God answered

"I am love. Follow me, call on me, and stay strong in your faith in me. You shall be rewarded in the love and light of God. Keep the faith in God."

Chapter 4

"You don't need to climb the highest mountain, or swim the deepest ocean. See me in a child's eyes so full of wonder, love and hope." -God

As we discuss the truth of God, you will understand how each opportunity in life is to let go of any negative thoughts, problems, or actions and therefore elevate your vibration and soul to connect you with your truest purpose, to be closer to God.

So, what is the truth of God?

It is not as black-and-white to explain. There are many facets to it. But what God is, God is unconditionally and unapologetically love. All-encompassing love.

God showed me the deeper truths, which are described in further detail under these five topics:

1. Religion
2. Poverty
3. Awareness/Self realization
4. Health
5. Death/Dying

These are all human experiences. So, to understand me, we must break down and dissect these human experiences to know who I truly am.

Religion:

Have you ever felt misplaced in church? The religion that you were told to follow and follow that one religion only.

What if I were to tell you that God doesn't care what religion you follow? God doesn't even care if you believe in God.

Pow! Bang! Mind blown.

In connecting with God, this is what I have seen about religion.

Religion can be a beautiful experience of humanity. It can bring faith, joy, and hope to those who are seeking. **There is NO right or wrong religion.** Let me say that again: **There is NO right or wrong religion.**

I asked, "Even atheism?"

Even atheism. Yes. Because within atheism people believe in the science of the world and how it was created from one organism in outer space, and they are so proud of knowing that. How can I take my love from their passions? I don't.

All religions are created equal. No right or wrong, as long as it is done with love, joy, and hope. It is all God, it is all part of me. Do not be afraid to explore and enjoy what life has to offer you. Understand and know mostly love *above all things. Love yourself; love your neighbor. I made human beings to have this vast diversity of cultures here on planet Earth.*

God makes me understand that any religion is completely part of our free will, but God wants it to be derived from love. If it is a religion that is led with the intention of causing hate or harm to yourself or others, then that's where God is not.

God's intention for us is to give humankind free will.

Free will is the ability to make choices here on Earth as we see fit. With every action, there is a reaction. This is why God wants us to love and be kind to one another in life and in our religious beliefs. When we start with hate, the reaction will be hateful. When we start with love, the reaction will be loving.

Why do we all have separate religions? Why is there not one faith that we all believe in? We all derive from Source, so why can't we have one faith in unison?

We are all made differently here on Earth to diversify and create a beautiful, diverse planet. All of our differences should not divide us but bring people together. Can't you see that having someone with values different from yours can help humankind and Mother Earth grow to a more elevated state? Our strengths are our differences, and we are all connected. We can use our differences to learn and grow intellectually, physically, and spiritually. All of our differences make us special with God's plan.

For example, you may not know how to connect Wi-Fi to your home database; I know I don't. However, you may have a neighbor who knows how to do that very well. So, this neighbor comes and sets up your Wi-Fi. You thank this neighbor by baking a pie. Your neighbor doesn't know how to bake but loves pie. So, you see how in this scenario, both two separate people came together with their differences to come to one solution. This is just one simple, beautiful vastness of how the world helps balance our diversities.

What I am trying to explain is that we are all vibrational beings, and the Earth has its own vibration, given by God.

The earth is humming and singing at this very moment. You

can't technically hear this humming, but it is there. When we come together and unify as one, we will lift our vibrations and collectively lift the vibration of the Earth.

Coming together cultivates a beautiful diversity that strengthens our knowledge, lifts humanity's vibrations, and connects us closer to God.

Just today, I was walking in Costco and feeling a little low. I passed a mother and a daughter; the daughter was about four years old. The daughter was being playful with her mom. She was grabbing her face and making her rub her nose, and the mom kept saying, "You are so silly." I couldn't help but notice them; as I did, they passed me. I noticed tingling on the top of my crown chakra at the top of my head. It was vibrating so quickly that I actually had to rub it. I went through the rest of my shopping feeling better and shared a smile with a couple of strangers.

This is the cause and effect: how this mother and daughter helped raise my vibration unintentionally. It was so innocent and sweet that I couldn't help but share it with the next person I came in contact with. So, we all have this affection for each other —a beautiful bond.

When we can lift our own vibrations through love, laughter, and be silly or whatever it may be. The world collectively joins in and raises its vibration with us; it's palpable. I want you to understand how powerful your actions are to you and the people around you. This is God wanting messages of love to heal yourself and others.

In religion, you can often find this battle between good and evil. God and the Devil. Well, with no evil and no Devil, how can religion tell you what is right or wrong? As I am connecting with God, this is considered blasphemy in some religions. Some religions believe one is not able to connect with God or to have such power. And since I am connecting with God, I will go straight to Hell. Or if I offend God, a righteous hand will come down and smite a striking blow to kill or do harm to me.

There is not a single word of this that is true. God has shown me that with an all-loving God, there is no such ridicule. Some may think that if something bad happens to someone, they can twist the reason being that they have sinned or done wrong in their life to God. Anything negative in our lives has been brought on through people's karmic reaction of negative cause and effect.

I am all love. Why would I make humankind have all the negative and positive emotions to have a vengeful reaction when something has gone wrong? I don't judge as much as humans judge themselves. Any negative actions cause chain reactions of negativity around that action. I don't wish for humans to cause harm or hate to each other, but I also don't interfere with free will.

This is all part of your experience here on Earth. What are you doing to do your part in helping Mother Earth? Are you taking care of yourself? Being kind to yourself? Are you taking care of others? Are you being kind to others? I understand that it is not always so easy to keep positive when someone has wronged you. But this is where you need to ask God for help. I can help you process and calm your emotional state to keep you more balanced and focused on what is good in the world.

I want religion to be something that excites you about life, brings joy to your heart, and opens your mind to the concept of how to reach me. You are all able to connect and hear me. Are you listening?

Sometimes a church or religion can get caught in the act of not deriving its foundation on love and religion, but more on the means of business and money. This is where corruption and greed come into play with religion.

God asked to address the negative effects of religion.

These derive from false human emotions that are as follows:

Fear

Greed

Lack of communication/understanding

Chapter 5

"Fear can hold you down from being your true self."
-God

Fear

"The unknown is the cause of fear instead of coming to an understanding about Earth's beautiful, diverse religions and cultures. Fear can cause division and hate. This is where I am not. I am not at the forefront of people's minds and hearts if fear is driving the wheel. They don't see God, and when they don't see me, it causes destruction, cruelty and war." -God

Some religions have elaborated false stories to add fear into the minds of humans. These elaborations are to rule out how humans should be perfect specimens in society. These religions want to instill this fear in their followers to have an unrealistic behavioral change in humanity. This is where I mostly struggled with the church myself. It has been hard for me to grasp that a God who loves me would want me to go to Hell if I have wronged God in any way.

One of these rules are sinning. To sin is defined as "an immoral act considered to be a transgression against the divine law". What God would make us with all love and give us free will but not love us if we sin? The list of sins in some religions can be pages long.

God said:

There is no sinning if love is in your heart. You can do no wrong as long as you love yourself and others, which in turn is to love me. Be kind to others as you would be kind to yourself. Any actions that would cause harm or hurt to you or others are not to sin, but they are a human experience, and I will never turn my back on a lost soul.

This means that if crimes are committed or other horrible acts are committed, God will always accept every being into God's kingdom or Heaven.

It is not my will that these actions be pursued, but I am always there to guide and help these souls. For they are also on a journey just like you.

I know we have already touched on this subject a bit, but you say there is Heaven; is there a Hell?

No. There is no physical place like Hell where there is a Devil to control it. This is part of adding fear to humankind so they will be a controlled society. However, sometimes, when a soul incarnates on Earth and lowers their vibration by doing hateful or harmful acts, it cannot hear me. Meaning that, in their life or their death, I am still here for them when I reach out to them. But by their own free will, they don't or can't hear me. Meaning they don't join me in Heaven, and they are stuck on the Earthly plane. They are stuck in their thoughts and emotions. This can be interpreted as a type of personal Hell. But there is no physical location. These souls can choose to come to Heaven and be with me.

Okay, let's discuss this a bit because this was a doozy.

What God has shown me is that if you believe in Hell and want to believe in Hell, then God says go for it. You don't need to change any of your views on what I am writing if that is not what you believe. I want you to understand that, again, there is no right or wrong religion as long as there is love and connection with God. Again, if it is not harmful or hateful to you or to others.

So, do you understand now that you can always go with God? God will always be there for you. Listen, if you do acts of "sin," there will be consequences in your life review after you die. And you will go through the feelings and emotions you negatively impacted someone in that action. I get it, so it is similar to God not wanting us to be mean or hateful to one another. So, if our actions align with negative actions, then there are consequences for them.

God states:

I reach out to them... But...they don't hear me.

When you act out of hate and fear, you lower your vibration. If that act leads you to die in that moment or even years down your lifetime, it can cause you to stay in a lower vibration. This is where your soul can feel damned, or maybe in Hell of some sort. Like I said, there is no physical place.

That is Hell, but God has shown me that people who lower their vibration a soul can get stuck here on Earth. So, in a sense, they can be in their own personal Hell.

If these souls choose to come to Heaven and be with me, they can.

These souls still have free will and can still go with God. It is just that sometimes they are so stuck on this low vibration that God is reaching out to them, and they cannot hear God. So, personally, if I were stuck where I couldn't go with God, it would feel like damnation.

Ok, moving on.

Some religions believe that there will be a second coming of Jesus; it will be an end of days or Armageddon of sorts.

Where the non-sinners will be rewarded and join Jesus in Heaven. Heaven is lovely, so I get the intrigue here, but Armageddon? Sorry to disappoint, but that is a fabricated tale in the Bible. It has been instilled to behave. Be a model citizen, and do not dare to have separate opinions, desires, or actions from what the church tells you. Lies, lies, and more lies.

God accepts and loves you for who you are, even with what you have done, and wants you to love yourself and others.

We need to move away from fear and step into love. We need to wake up and understand that our souls are ancient beings of different vibrational frequencies that have a lesson to learn here on Earth. The main lesson is to learn, teach, grow, and heal in love. This is how your soul ascends.

This is where you find the Truth in God.

Chapter 6

"You understand me more, when you have nothing."
-God

Greed

Greed is another derivative of human emotion in religion. It is driven by desires for money, power, sex, etc. Greed, along with fear, can be the number one reason humans have war. Let's say that again: Greed and fear can be the number one reason humans have war. To be greedy is to be selfish, so when someone is greedy, they exude the feeling of love towards others. They only have a hypersensitive love for themselves or a physical monetary item.

Power + Greed = Hate

Humans need to learn that there are no material needs to get them closer to God. Greed will pull you further away from God. There is no emotion when greed is at the forefront of a person's actions. No room for empathy, and no room for love. They become blindsided by the focus of that one thing and one thing only. Money is a thing that has become necessary here on earth for the exchange of goods, but what do you really need in life?

When you suddenly become terminally ill, do you think of how much money you have in your bank account? Or do you think of your loved ones? Do you think of possibly someone you may have hurt in the past and would like to make things right? This is a small glimpse of how a life review is processed, which is discussed in a later chapter. Earth is a school. We are here to learn and grow in love.

We are discussing all the negative attributes that can come from a religion. Greed can be seen in religions and churches around us. I don't know about you, but I am all set at the church, where the priest is driving in a G-wagon. I don't want to be involved in a church, where the money received from its recipients helps the church congregation get richer. The Vatican is sitting on a gold mine, for goodness sake.

This does not mean forsaking or leaving a church because I am making you aware of these things. It's just to help you on your spiritual journey to know that God loves you for all the parts of who you are, not how much money you donate to a church.

You don't need to enter a church to pray and connect with God. God wants you to do whatever feels good in your soul. So, if you feel a deep-rooted connection in attending church, then great! Keep doing what feels good to you. That is where you are meant to be, then.

I am writing this book because God wants me to speak the truth. So, there is no sugarcoating here. Don't think that if you miss one day of church, you are sent straight to damnation; that will never happen.

God knows you at your soul level, and you don't need to prove anything to God or to anyone else.

Do what makes your heart sing.

Chapter 7

"Speak the truth, and it will set you free." -God

Lack of communication/understanding

This is where we can combine fear and greed because we may not understand another person for how or why they do things either in their daily rituals and religious practices.

Sometimes, we need to reach out to one another and inquire about the reasons why one person does something versus another.

This is about connecting with people to understand their differences.

Ask questions and understand what makes us different in our cultural and religious beliefs. When we unify, we will move into a more enlightened space together. We will become enlightened, and the earth will shift into enlightenment together. To be enlightened in the spiritual sense is to have the all-knowing and full consciousness of how the universe and God work.

The Atlantians, the people of Atlantis, were enlightened beings. They were light beings who had a collective purpose of living harmoniously together and with the Earth.

I asked if Atlantis was a real place.

Atlantis was a real place on Earth.

Atlantis was a beautiful place where water flowed all around the entire city. Atlantians used this water to make a power source and to help their colony strengthen and prosper. This water provided life to the plants that they consumed and water to the Atlantians.

These enlightened beings understood how everything in nature is connected to us. They used a power source, crystal energy, that was given to them through otherworldly galactic beings. The Atlantians looked at this power as a divine energy source. God connects all beings together to help civilizations grow in their own evolution.

Atlantis came to an end when greed took over some of its population. The light crystal source that derived their power of cultivation was being compromised. The flood was set in their timeline to rid themselves of greed. Only some selective high beings and their power source were saved.

Atlantians were not the only divine-driven civilization in history. The Mayans built massive structures and highly complex cities within the jungles of Central America.

We are all unique creatures of God. While on this Earth, we need to learn to love each other's differences and communicate to bring humankind closer together and, more importantly, closer to God.

Chapter 8

Poverty:

To delve into the deeper truth of God, one needs to understand having nothing. This does not mean that God wants you to go through poverty. But God wants you to reflect and strip everything you have away: money, cars, and material items. What are you left with? Do you curse God when you are down and out, or is this where you find your faith in God? If everything in your life went precisely to plan, would you ever call on God? God does not mean for you to suffer, but more to understand the full grasp of reality. There is no right or wrong; there just is.

If you have nothing but your loved ones, family, spouse, son, daughter, etc., you have everything. And that is where you have faith in God. Do not want in excess; understand the subtleties of life. Be still to understand and know God is with you.

A soul's journey can be hard on this planet. It is the most challenging across many galaxies. You, like I, have chosen this life with every stepping stone along the way. We chose our friends, our family, our children. We chose around the time we will marry or if we will marry. All of this is written and understood before we are even born. If you find that you are struggling in any aspect of your life, reflect on why your soul would have chosen this journey for you.

What is the lesson here? How can you overcome these hardships? What must be done? When you have faith, any hardships can be overcome. It can be very difficult to keep the faith.

A man who has lost everything thinks that his life is over. But to have a man with a fresh perspective, this fresh perspective is knowing you have life; this is the righteousness of understanding God. The power that is within you. You have to activate this power by believing in yourself and pursuing your passions. Faith can waiver, but that doesn't mean God waivers. I am always here for you. In your good times and bad times.

How long have we been away from Heaven? Do we brush that memory away, or do we keep the faith and know that we will reunite with God in Heaven again? One small step at a time: keep the faith.

Chapter 9

"You are worthy of Love." -Virgin Mary

Awareness/Self Realization:

Who are you? No, who are you really? You are not just a lawyer, a nurse, or a contractor. Who are you deep down in your soul? What have you been brought to this earth to do? Some may not find the answer to these questions in this lifetime. Each soul has the same purpose from God's perspective: to be kind and love yourself and others. This is how we love God. God wants you to understand that knowing yourself and being true to who you are is one of the first steps to reaching your soul enlightenment journey. It is hard to not always fit the mold of who or what society wants you to be.

For example, your mother has always wanted you to become a family physician and follow in your father's footsteps. But you have always had a yearning to help animals—a veterinarian perhaps. But you push that thought away because it would shame your family greatly. But why? Why would you deny that this is where you are being called? When we have these inner thoughts and deep desires, this is a glimpse into our soul's contract here on Earth. This is what we are called to do.

If for example, they choose the family physician path, there will be a lot of depression and anxiety, maybe even hatred, because they did not listen to their true calling. And it is always a calling if it is for the highest good of yourself and humanity. Keep kindness throughout. When you shift into your true, authentic self, every aspect of your life will be better: better relationships, no depression, and living with joy and purpose.

This does not mean that you have to quit your job tomorrow. But listen to that intuitive guide that your innermost self has been guiding you to do. Be open to the possibilities around you because once you become self-aware, God will make a positive ripple effect happen for you.

Even if it's just a subtle acknowledgment, the universe will align you with that purpose. The universe will cut ties with people or places you weren't supposed to be with, and it will open new opportunities for you.

God is so happy and excited when you find out more about why you are here on this Earth at this very time.

Step into your role, and you will come into the light.

Chapter 10

Health:

When you have a drastic health change in your life, who do you turn to? Do you call your loved ones, be that family or friends? Because that is what matters most in life.

You will call to them as you will call to me. And I will be there for you. I am with you always. Every beat of your heart is a reminder that I gave you life. I am always with you.

Remember the poem of the footprints in the sand?

'Footprints in the Sand

One night, I dreamed of walking along the beach with the Lord. Scenes from my life flashed across the sky. In each, I noticed footprints in the sand. Sometimes, there were two sets of footprints; other times, there was only one.

During the low periods of my life, I could see only one set of footprints, so I said, "You promised me, Lord, that you would walk with me always. Why have you not been there for me when I have needed you most?"

The Lord replied, *"The times when you have seen only one set of footprints, my child is when I carried you."*

As I carry you now. When your soul is ready, I will call you home.

God has not forsaken you. God has been with you all along. The times that you are struggling the most and your faith can waiver, God is still there, carrying you along the way and guiding you on your true path. There have been many times that I have thought God has forgotten about me, that I was wandering through this life without anyone to turn to.

Even though I didn't know my faith was being tested through my trials and tribulations, it helps me more now than ever that I have lived through those times because when you come out of it onto the other side, all you see is the glory of God. And what God has laid before you.

You had to overcome obstacles to better understand yourself and your relationship with God.

Chapter 11

Death and Dying:

Humans think differently about death and dying than other galactic beings. They grieve. Grieving is the overwhelming sadness you feel as a human when a loved one passes away. There can be happiness and joy found within that pain, too. There is no right or wrong way to die. The universe understands the balance of everything when a single soul transitions from Earth into Heaven. It's similar to the Earth's ecosystem. The world is beautiful; think of the lush forest with tall trees, grass underneath, and moss. The leaves of the trees will fall to the Earth (symbolizing death) in autumn, giving the soil new life (rebirth). It will enrich the soil to bring out flowers that will bloom in the springtime. So, you see, the universe does not feel sad for this leaf, but it sees the beauty of this leaf, giving life and moving its energy in another way. That is similar to how death works.

When a person dies, a new life grows somewhere else on the planet. This balance can be beautiful, but it is very hard to see when a person is grieving. But know that your loved ones always go with God and feel safe and at peace on the other side.

Dying is a very personal journey. People still have free will when they die. They cannot "crossover" until they have fully accepted to do so. Now, understandably, that is not the case for everyone. There is trauma or other factors that come into play that can cause a soul to leave quickly or tragically. Because of this trauma, you may think that a soul did not use their free will. But indeed, it is contracted prior to their birth of how they will die. Dying is one of the biggest agreements on your life contract. It can be difficult to think; for example, my mother didn't choose to get murdered or my brother didn't choose to get into a fatal car crash. But what happens is their soul knows before being born how their life will impact others in a positive or negative way.

Because of this, they will choose the time of death to either give life elsewhere or to be on the other side to give and help others.

You are fully aware of all of this in Heaven. Your soul understands the cause and effect of your own passing. Sometimes, life is just too hard for some here on Earth, and they choose to go home early. That's okay.

God says

I will always be there for them.

God, what happens when we die?

The soul carries on and joins with me in the place you call Heaven. The soul will initially sense everything around them is different. Not every soul travels into the light immediately. Some choose to stay with their earthly body or loved ones for some time. Remember, they still have free will and can choose when to start the soul's journey back home.

Then, the light is shown to the soul, showing how to return to Heaven. This light is so beautiful and shows the soul with love, comforting them along the way. I designed it to remind them of where they are actually from and to keep them calm on their transition since, let's face it, the beginning of the end can sometimes be confusing to the soul. There is not only light, but sometimes soft music playing. This adds to the ambiance to create a smooth transition. All the senses can be used at this point. There can also be a soft, beautiful smell, perhaps a scent of rose. It's all very personal to you, but most souls share a similar experience.

Then, the soul will enter a waiting room of sorts, where it will be greeted by its loved ones who have passed before it in this lifetime. This is such a happy moment for a soul to be reunited with loved ones that it has thought that it had lost on Earth.

Excuse me, I'm sorry to cut in, but what do you mean by they thought that they lost?

You can interrupt me anytime. I am happy to answer all questions that you may have. When souls reside on Earth as human beings, they can forget where they are truly from and where a soul goes when we pass. See, not everyone on Earth believes in God and, therefore, does not believe in Heaven. So, when a soul passes, some believe they will never be reunited with them again. But that is not true. A soul will always be reunited with the loved ones that it lost here on Earth. But they are never truly lost; those souls whom have passed can always be around the people who stay on Earth for a little while longer. Some people do believe in an afterlife, and sometimes those who do not can sense and feel their loved ones around. They will get a whiff of their perfume or a butterfly of their favorite color lands directly in their view, and they will think of their lost loved one. This is no coincidence. Souls from Heaven send these things to remind their loved ones that they are at peace and with God.

So, I want to return to how a soul returns home to Heaven and what happens after they are reunited in this waiting room after the soul recently crosses over.

Then, when the soul is ready, their spiritual team, also known

47

as spirit guides, will greet the soul and ask when they are ready. The soul can then process the life review. The life review is a process where every action and word spoken to each individual or animal will be shown to you as a full immersion experience. It's almost like reliving the moments of your full lifetime, but sometimes, feeling only processed in a few minutes. This experience will let the soul feel how they made other people or animals feel with each interaction. The soul can then process where things might not have been the kindest interaction or need improvements to help heal the soul by always keeping God and love at the forefront of everything you do. After the life review, there is a scrubbing of the soul, almost like an eternal shower. It is very enjoyable for the soul; it rids the soul of burdens carried from this lifetime and washes them away, so to speak. But there is no need for a soul to physically have a shower. Just to remind you, though, a soul can do anything in Heaven as it has done on Earth. Shower, exercise, sex.

Really sex?

Really, sex.

So, when the soul is cleansed and ready, then they sit with their assigned group of souls that are equal to their vibration and will start school and learning. There is never enough for a soul to grow and learn. And it isn't a tedious task for a soul. The soul always loves to learn and gets excited about its classes and seeing its so-called classmates each time. When classes aren't in session or whenever the soul chooses, it can go off and experience the great vastness of our universe and beyond. It can explore other planets. The soul can go back and visit Earth to see loved ones that they have left behind. There is always, always free will. You do not lose that as a soul when you cross into Heaven. If anything, you have more of the awakened soul and greatly understand this in Heaven. You can use it to your advantage by playing around and experiencing your soul's life here.

Heaven is amongst you right now. Most of you cannot sense or see it, but it is on a plane that is neither above nor below you—it's almost transverse. It's like it goes through your world. This is where it weaves as a plane that has no limitations of Earth. It is a beautiful, wondrous place for souls to experience more than they could ever dream of.

I always pictured Heaven above us. Even when I raise my vibration to enter a meditation or a reading, I feel my energy lift upward.

That would be because your vibrational frequency is lifting higher. But Heaven is amongst you right now. It's almost as if you stepped into a doorway and just went left.

Huh? Just went left.

Exactly. It's not as complicated and as far away as some may seem. It is all around you, almost encompassing you. Like a warm hug. Cozy up with me anytime you would like; I will always be the warm hug you need.

Chapter 12

After we die, we are immediately taken to a place where we cleanse our souls to shed any earthly connections here on Earth. I'm telling you, you are going to love it. It's like when you go camping and haven't showered in days and finally have that first shower. It is glorious; you are bathed and cleansed. Once you have completed that step, you are moved to an area where you can sit and have your life reviewed with your spirit guides.

Your spirit guides are otherworldly beings that are connected with you and always help guide you on your journey here on Earth. Spirit guides will help you set up everything that will be happening this lifetime before you are even born on this planet. It is all written and kept in your scrolls in the Akashic records. Akashic records are the location where all the soul's previous and current life contracts are kept and made.

I have been to the Akashic records through meditations and or medium/psychic readings.

I want to take a moment and describe to you what I "see" in my meditations when I go to the Akashic records. My first experience at the Akashic Records, I wasn't even sure I would be able to get there or go. I asked my spirit guides for help. I can't remember which spirit guide helped me, but I had my group of 14 guides and I asked, "Can you please take me to the Akashic records?"

I'm not sure which of my guides did it, but I felt a gentle grab of my hand, and whoosh, we flew up and up, and it felt very far and distant. But we were there in less than 5 seconds flat. As I peered around, I felt like everything was surrounded by these soft, white, pillowy clouds. My guide held my hand through the whole experience. As far as my eyes could see, there were rows and rows of ancient texts and scrolls. Some books were leather bound with the spine facing out. Others were tattered and were scrolls of sorts, just rolled papers stuffed in between. It was all very organized; I was observing the book's differences, admiring all the shapes and sizes. Nothing was bright in color, or one stuck out more than the rest.

Everything looked a very neutral tone of browns and beiges.

I didn't see anyone else that was at the Akashic records. I know some claim that there is a keeper of these records.

Maybe it was because I was already with my guide, but I was able to grab whatever book or scroll I wished off of these shelves. In this space, I have gone back many times to help read past lives for me or my clients. The Akashic records are a place of learning. It is a library of sorts of who you are and who you have been. It will tell you the greatest challenges you have faced in your lifetimes repeatedly or your biggest achievements. It is all there.

Most of the time, when I read the Akashic records to clients or myself, it has not been a life that they have lived here on Earth. Often, it is their life that they have lived on another planet. Which makes it so much more fascinating. I have read an elf-like woman that almost had an iridescent glow to her skin, she was so beautiful. I have also had the privilege of reading someone's records from a water world of sorts. Where everyone was mermaids.

Every soul has had different reincarnations and different life experiences. That is the beauty of a specific soul's journey: to experience life, all life, on different planets as different beings.

Chapter 13

Since we just finished discussing how the soul moves through death and dying. I wanted to ask specifically about reincarnation. Can you explain it to me? Is it real?

Well, of course it is real. It is as real as your soul itself.

*Reincarnation is the soul's journey of returning to a planet that it chooses. So, you have come to Earth many times over. This is **only** by your choice, your free will.*

It is not of God's will. You choose to reincarnate to either learn, play, or grow, all with love. This is very empowering to a soul to have the choice of when and where to go. I always enjoy the excitement I will feel of the soul getting to return to another life on Earth.

You see, stepping into a new journey for a soul in the soul realm/Heaven is so exciting. A soul is not scared of the unknown; the unknown is exhilarating to them as they think of all the personal encounters they will have and all the places they will go. It is not all unknown, though. Most of each lifetime you have on Earth is prewritten—a soul contract, if you will.

This is discussed and processed prior to your return to Earth with your spiritual team of guides. You lay out all of the careers you may have. Where you will live. Who will be in your family, soul family. Reincarnation is a beautiful gift that is enjoyed and cherished.

Some believe that reincarnation is a burden. It is quite the opposite. There is only love, excitement, and joy when a soul gets to reincarnate. *In the current present that you live in, though, there are still worldwide problems that aren't resolved. Famine, war, hate, just to name a few. And if your current life feels negative or you don't have your dream life or are struggling. Only through the struggle and having nothing, can you come through the other side with complete joy and admiration for yourself and others.*

We have discussed this before, but in the struggle is where you look for God. I am always with you, never leaving your side. Your perseverance will change your life completely. The smallest stepping stone can get you on the right path. Say you are a beggar on the street. You have no money, no food, and no shelter. You find at night that it is cold —too cold —without a jacket or blanket. Do you sit still and think well, I will just sit here and freeze to death? Or do you start walking, a so-called journey to find a warm place or warm blanket?

As you walk, I am with you. I am guiding you step by step. By taking that initiative that puts the limitless power of the universe in your hands, you have now set in motion a chain reaction. You come to a gas station where the clerk may be closing up for the evening. You ask if you can quickly use the restroom. They say, "Sure." You go in to use the restroom, and when you finish, you say goodbye to the clerk.

The clerk says, "Hey, it's pretty cold outside tonight. Do you have anything to keep you warm?"

You answer, "No." The clerk says, "Well, I don't have much, but I have a blanket in the back of my car that I can give you." This is like gold to you—to have something to keep you warm, to keep you going. And it all started with struggling and taking that first step.

That story is full of hope and kindness; I loved it.

I know; that's why I told it to you. There is so much more love in humanity than people give it credit for. A lot of people choose to see the bad in the world. This is not how I want them to enjoy their lives. I want them to live, laugh often, and love fully. This is the whole reason for reincarnation: to play a new role in this thing called life. Have fun, experience joy, and share love often. Hold it in your heart always.

How many times have I been to Earth?

Thousands.

Doesn't that seem like I haven't learned the lesson I am supposed to have learned? Isn't it a soul's journey just to stay in Heaven?

You have chosen to come and return to Earth thousands of times because you want to play and have fun. It is meant to be more of an experience. You can learn along the way. As you do learn, your body will become clearer about who you really are at your soul level.

You are a highly sensitive vibrational being who has reincarnated on Earth and on other planets as well. You can choose to stay in Heaven as long as you wish, but I see it time and time again that a soul will choose to reincarnate because, for a lack of better terms, gets bored.

When you are closer to connecting to the true essence of your soul while on Earth, it helps you lift your vibration to get closer to God. Ascension to God is what all souls strive to achieve.

You have said this before. Ascending your vibration to get closer to God is part of our souls' journey. But if we reincarnate on Earth for fun, then isn't there no journey to achieve?

I think what you are trying to ask is if it is the soul's purpose.

54

Of course, raising your vibration to be closer to God is the soul's purpose. But being human on Earth is about the experience. It can aide and rapidly increase you as a vibrational being to ascend to God. But being human is not your purpose; it is just an experience.

Sometimes, people get caught up in wishing away moments to the next thing. Remind yourself to live in the present and to take in and enjoy this lifetime that is all around you.

Chapter 14

"There is no burden too great or small, for with God all things are possible." - God

Forgiveness has so much power in the universe, and this chapter explains how it works. How do we forgive and let go when someone has hurt or wronged us in some way? The answer is simple: Send them forgiveness.

You can just say it in your head to yourself, out loud, or directly to the person who has wronged you. There is immense power when you give and receive forgiveness when someone has hurt you. This means to forgive the most horrendous acts and abusers. This helps your soul heal in many ways and opens pathways to your health, well-being, and overall success. Yes, because you haven't done this practice of forgiveness, that is why you are stuck in an endless loop of woe and self-pity or doubt. Also, it will hold you back from reaching your goals in life. It can also cause illness within your body by holding onto negative energy that your body so desperately needs you to let go of.

This is about forgiveness in others and, more importantly, in yourself. How do you even start to heal?

How do you heal wounds that others may have inflicted on you, if you have not forgiven yourself? Do you truly love yourself? Do you hold yourself in the highest regard?

Forgive yourself. This allows love to flow and energy to heal those emotional wounds. Emotional wounds can be just as damaging as physical wounds, and any sickness can be caused by emotional trauma.

Have you forgiven yourself? Have you forgiven your abuser?

The body and mind of humans are designed by God to be their own healers. You just have to understand your power. And forgiveness sets up huge shifts in your spiritual, physical, and mental well-being. Picture an energetic cord between you and the abuser and cut it. As you do this, say, "I forgive you...and I forgive myself." You will notice things align in your life more precisely. Success, love, and healing will come your way. When you offer this forgiveness, your soul sheds this negative energy that is holding you down from goals and being happy in your life.

When the soul sheds this negative energy, your soul lifts its vibration in return, and you will be more in line with who you are and who your soul is meant to be here on Earth. You will allow more room in your mind, body, and spirit for positive growth and, most importantly, love.

To forgive yourself is to love yourself. To forgive others is to love others. Love is an essential part of God and our souls.

It is not easy to forgive thine enemy.

Where does someone even start?

With forgiving themselves first. Not all circumstances, but those situations where a person has been wronged by someone else, they will put shame on themselves. The victim will play different scenarios in their head with different outcomes. But really, is there a victim at all? It is seen from all perspectives on all timelines, past and present. Someone who was sexually abused as a child grew older and started to sexually abuse others who were small as well. Does God hold haste or send this soul to damnation? No.

There is no wrongdoing on Earth that God does not know or see. I do not want negative actions on Earth for people as a society. But also, I do not interfere with free will. And this abuser only knew how to be an abuser because of his or her past. There is no damnation. I know this can be hard to grasp for some, but it is all understood in a karmic wheel of negative and positive causes and effects on Earth.

Not every human experience is a positive one. This is because a soul has to experience tragedy before being released to the positive light of God. Let me explain more deeply. At the soul level, there is no right or wrong; there just is. The omnipresent or fifth-dimensional theories of whatever has happened before are happening now and in the future. So, for a soul to have this negative experience is only to lead the way for more positivity in all the timelines before and after.

I'm not sure if I fully grasp this concept. Can you explain it in another way?

Of course. Look at a heart rate monitor hooked up to an EKG. You understand that rhythm, that perfect rhythm that gives you a life. The air that you are breathing, the beautiful sunrise.

What you are seeing is all because your heart is beating in perfect rhythm. When reading an EKG, these are called waves; they are the beautiful rhythm of the blood moving in and out of the heart.

Blood moving out is an example of the negative, death and dying because, without blood, there would be no life. Then, in another contraction of the heart, the blood fills the ventricles, and life is restored.

This example shows how when you think nothing is happening, everything is happening for life to happen. Even though this downward spike is almost reflective of death and dying, it's not. It is giving life but adding the blood back in. And then the cycle *continues to solely give life. There will always be a negative reaction in life. It is how your soul chooses to evolve and move forward that is the reaction. You always have the choice.*

But always know that God is giving you a life.

Chapter 15

Life can be overwhelming; it can be really hard. To listen to the guidance that you are getting from God, you have to do three things:

1. Clear your mind
2. Cleanse your body
3. Comprehend

Clear your mind

The first step to listening to God is to clear your mind.

But how do we do that in a society that is so overloaded with social media? Phones? Television? This new-age technology is great, but it also has many downfalls. Most people have issues quieting their own minds without using one of these tools.

We are so busy in our lives. When do you ever take an hour or even 30 minutes to unplug and unwind?

A step-by-step process is used to clear your mind. First, start in a quiet space that is comfortable for you. Sit or lie down comfortably. Grab a blanket or pillow to make you feel secure. Start with grounding yourself. Grounding is the process of reconnecting with the Earth in order to promote healing. Use your imagination and imagine roots coming out of your feet and going deep into the Earth. This is grounding. If you can't picture it, it's okay. Sometimes, being outside barefoot will naturally ground you. Or just ask your body to do it for you, and it will. There is no need to get upset if you can't picture anything; just trust in your individual way of doing things.

Next, you will concentrate on your breathing. Take a few deep breaths. Sometimes, it helps if you count in for 3... 1,2,3 and out 1,2,3. Repeat this until you are thinking of only your breath. This is how you can clear your mind. This is step one of connecting with God.

If you cannot quiet your mind by sitting, try doing it while walking or on a treadmill—whatever works for you.

This is where your headspace needs to be to connect and hear God's guidance for you. You can also ask for signs from God—for example, show me a red cardinal today with a yellow flower if I am to accept this job, and let me have that all-knowingness when I see this sign. Thank you. Gratitude is huge, and we are going to talk about that in another chapter.

Chapter 16

Cleanse your body

God made our bodies these powerful vessels to heal and take care of themselves. However, you were born perfect. Our body impedes our mind from being clear of thought. If you are harmful to your body through substance abuse or bad nutrition, not giving your body enough sleep. There isn't a way that will help you clear your mind to understand God and what God is saying to you. If you aren't taking care of yourself physically, you will be sick often and experience fatigue or lethargy.

This is where God wants you to be your best version of yourself and clear your body of toxic foods and waste you don't need.

To understand and operate your body, you need to give your body the necessary space to create space for your intuition and for me to come in and connect with you. If there is abuse on the body, through substance or food, you will create brain fog and not be able to hear correctly. This Earth was made for you to have complete medicinal and nutritional needs throughout. Gardening and raising your own chickens for poultry and eggs, for example, holds much more nutrient value than anything you are able to buy in the store. For look at what the chickens eat in a poultry plant, processed pellets that sometimes have a chemically inducing agent to help keep the birds from getting disease. A chicken raised in your backyard, if able to roam, will eat all sorts of grubs, ticks, and insects. *This will give the chickens a higher nutrient diet, which will give you a more nutrient-produced egg or meat.*

See how the cycle of life is all around. What happens to one thing will have a similar karmic reaction to another. This example is related to food and where it comes from. Eating organically and not indulging in processed foods will cleanse your body and free it of limitations when you want to connect with me.

I am always here, guiding you and talking with you. You have to take the steps to follow me, and one of those steps is making sure you are getting everything you need to stay healthy and mentally sharp.

Chapter 17

Comprehend

This is where you have been able to cleanse your body and clear your mind, and now you can fully comprehend what God is saying to you. You need to have full trust in yourself, knowing that you are "hearing" God for the first time, and it is exciting.

You are not crazy, and yes, it will be in your minds voice, which I admit takes some time to get used to. But you are doing it; you are the perfect being and have good things to share with others. God will guide you on where you need to go. You just have to trust your gut instinct and what is being communicated to you. Sometimes, you can feel tingling, hear, or feel vibrating on your head or anywhere in your body. Just trust the process. It is completely set to who you are as an individual. I am so excited for you to connect with God and the Divine because it means you have come into this knowledge of lifting your vibration and being enlightened.

Chapter 18

"Let us rise up and be thankful, for if we didn't learn a lot today, at least we learned a little, and if we didn't learn a little, at least we didn't get sick, and if we got sick, at least we didn't die; so, let us all be thankful."
– Buddha

Gratitude is a huge way to lift your vibration here on Earth. This includes sharing gratitude with someone else or gratitude towards God and the Divine for good things that will happen or do happen in your life. It also includes sending out a big, honest thank you to God for sending you your dream job or finding the love of your life. This will only keep you more connected with God and stay on your true path here on Earth.

Even if this hasn't happened just yet, ask the Universe for exactly what you want and always express gratitude for it coming into your life. This is really the essential step for manifestation. To manifest something in your life is to picture and bring whatever it may be into fruition through the process of picturing it in your mind.

Sometimes, when good things happen to us, we forget to send that quick little thank you to God, the universe, and the divine or spirit guides. Don't forget this crucial step.

As I spoke earlier of the ripple effect through the universe. Sending gratitude will make huge waves, keeping all good and positive things flowing effortlessly into your life. God wants you to be happy in life, and you can have everything. You have to ask the right questions, follow your true path, and always express gratitude.

God says it is all yours for the taking.

Chapter 19

God wants you to live your most fulfilling life. Full of joy, love, and peace.

Chapter 20

Now that you have read and heard insights from God, here is a little conversation going back to the beginning of my connection with God. We will conclude God's teaching for this book because I feel like it has the strongest message for everyone to keep with them.

Here is what I wrote to God:

Sometimes I get so confused about what you are trying to say.

You are learning how to listen to me. Your mind is distracted and thinking of other things, such as dinner and the kids.

Can you help me hear you better?

Yes, I can come closer so you can hear me better.

Thank you. Ok, so what do you need me to write:

The Truth of God.

Well, sheesh, that seems like a big responsibility. Don't get me wrong; I am grateful. I am just trying to come to terms with everything. And I also don't know if little old me feels worthy of such responsibility.

You are worthy. This is the last lesson you really need to understand.

I want you to hold yourself in the highest regard. You are perfect with all of your imperfections. You only become a better person by understanding your self-worth. Why wouldn't it be you I connect with? I connect and speak with every one of my children. The ones who are listening are my messengers. There will be a time when there is no difference between someone connecting with themselves and connecting with God.

This is the human evolution and experience that I am trying to help guide people to.

To know you are worthy is to accept and love yourself fully.
To love yourself is to love God.

I love you. Thank you, for always guiding us.

I love you most.

Chapter 21

I am worthy of love
I am worthy of abundance
I am worthy of health
I am worthy of friends

~The Virgin Mary

Chapter 22

The Virgin Mary

Whenever I am in the presence of the Virgin Mary, she has this wonderful, calming presence. She is nurturing and soft in her words and communicating. The Virgin Mary will often have a red rose for me, or I have also had her shower me with rose petals. She wears a light blue tunic and a veil. In the following conversation I had with the Virgin Mary after channeling God, God said she wanted to say some things. Here is what she said:

I am so glad you are listening now.

You see, Mary has been trying to get my attention daily for some months now. But like I have mentioned before, connecting with the Divine, they always seem to speak in riddles and mention the same things over and over. So, she would always come to me in the late evening when I had finally sat down from a long day, and she would try talking with me. And I always felt too exhausted to chat, but how do you shrug away the Divine? Now that I realized I needed to connect with her and write it down for a book, I could hear her.

I then asked Mary, "How can I help you?"

You are helping; you are going to speak to the people.

Speak what exactly?

Speak what you know and what comes to your heart.

The truth about church and religion?

Yes, yes.

Teach them about hatred and greed. To be human is to have these emotions; to be a spirit is to know these emotions.

To be human is to have these emotions; and to be a spirit is to know these emotions.

Thank you, Mary, for always being with me.

I love you, my child.

I love you, too.

What else do I need to know?

You walk in the light of God, as do your brothers and sisters. People want to know your story. They want to know that you are like them and that they are all connected and one with God. You are no more special than the person to your left. Continue along your path.

Is it okay for me to talk about aliens?

*Intergalactic beings are connected to God as you are connected to God. You all come from the same source. God is the source of everything. God is unwavering and unassuming love. The purest and holiest love of all. You are God, and God is you. Saying the word "Aliens" is an earthly term. You are **all beings** of God. You are all sources of love, light, and vibrational energies.*

Do I speak of Hell?

What is Hell? There is no such place. There is no Hell or Heaven; only the space with God exists.

What do you mean by that exactly?

There is no Hell, meaning there is no place controlled by a Devil. There is no ongoing Divine war between good and evil. There is no such thing. And there is no Heaven because the place with God is just is. If you would like to call it Heaven, then that's okay. If you would like to believe that there is a Hell, then that's okay, too.

I come to you because I need you to guide people on their way. What you do in your daily life does not matter, but what you do for others will bring your soul closer to God, which is the purpose of our souls.

Mother Mary, you are so beautiful.

Well, if I am beautiful and we are both made by God, then you are beautiful as well.

What else do I need to know tonight?

You are connecting with the Divine, and you are to use this gift to speak to others.

In my mediumship?

Yes, in a way.

Do you want me to connect with you more directly?

Yes. You are a channeler of the Divine. You are an ascended master who can help humanity on Earth shift its consciousness and vibration.

But I am just one person.

There are many like you, and you can all work together.

OK.

The day this conversation took place was a cloudy, rainy day. As we were concluding our chat for this particular day, the sun came out and shone so brightly that I cried, knowing it was a message from Mary.

Mary, what would you like the readers of this book to know?

We will start with the small things of loving yourself and others around you. I have told you that you have always been connecting

74

with the Divine. *Loving yourself sounds like the simplest task, but for most people, this is not easy. We have to truly understand ourselves and who we want to be. And when I say be, I do not mean do. What a person does and who they are can be very different.*

I want you all to do an exercise. Go to the mirror and say out loud to yourself, "Who am I?" If you don't get an answer, try again tomorrow, the next day, the next day, and so on. When you do get an answer, please write it down. You don't have to understand it fully right away, but I know it will be the start of you aligning your true self with the person you are today.

Keep trying, and don't give up on yourself. Most people don't have enough faith in themselves.

To doubt yourself is to doubt the Divine.

Chapter 23

Hi Mary.

Hello, kind soul.

What do you want to talk about today, Mary?

You are connecting to the Divine. You will give hope to those who need it.

Thank you.

You are enough. You all are enough. Worthiness is a cause to break boundaries.

What is that supposed to mean?

Don't worry about what others may think of you. Walk your own true path, for I am walking beside you. Keep your chin up and your head held high. (spoken like a true mother)

How do you feel being the mother of Jesus?

Blessed and humbled. I, too, didn't feel worthy. I knew I was given a great challenge as well, and I was doubted by so many. I wavered in my faith at times, but I knew I had to fulfill my prophecy. I felt scared and alone at times, but Joseph was strong and willing to support me through it all. I was so grateful for him, baby Jesus, and God blessed me with this gift. I was indeed a virgin and was given the blessing of bearing a child, Jesus.

What do you want people to know about your journey?

I struggled too. I had to find my own way and walk blindly in my faith in God. Keep walking, one step at a time, and you, too, can fulfill your destiny.

What do our destinies look like now?

To keep God at the forefront of what they do. Because they will be the enlightened ones to walk through the dark and emerge into the basking glory of God's light.

How can we help in our daily lives?

Walk in God's faith, especially when it seems like God has failed you. Understand the greater picture of the universe and the exchange necessary.

What do you mean by exchange?

The perfect balance of the universe is charged by positive and negative ions, energies, and experiences. Don't you see? The gift of God is to know God in the unseen.

I believe I'm still confused.

Look at the ant. One small ant cannot survive on its own. It relies on its colony to bring food when it cannot. Every ant has a critical role to play in the survival of its colony. When an ant dies, the other ants do not grieve; they understand the balance of the positive and negative experiences necessary for the beautiful balance of life.

How am I to help the people of Earth?

You are to write this story of your conversations with me. People need to know I have not forsaken them. I am here for the children of God.

That is beautiful; thank you, Mary.

Thank you for listening.

Chapter 24

"Give love, receive love, be love."
-Virgin Mary

Hello, my child. There is a lot of unrest in the world currently. War is not something the Divine likes to see on planet Earth. The Divine cannot stop war because it is from human hatred and greed. If God were truly in their hearts, war would never exist. There is always free will of the people.

Is there a way for humanity to stop war from happening?

Show kindness, even if it's just to you or your spouse. Positive energy (and hatred) has ripple effects that profoundly affect the Earth and the Universe.

Like the scene from the movie Pocahontas, where grandmother Willow dips her vine into the river, it creates ripples. She says, 'So small at first, then look how they grow. But someone has to start them.' This is positivity, and it causes a chain reaction of positive ripples.

The Divine cannot intervene on free will, but we show signs and aide in what should and could be done. One sign is in synchronicities being shown 11:11 over and over again — this could change an outcome for a political leader who listens to the guidance that is being given to them by the Divine. Or a cardinal on their porch, which is a positive, uplifting sign to make them pause, think, and not act harshly.

Will there be a war in 2024?

Yes, but war will end indefinitely when humankind has come to an understanding of the greater purpose of their souls. To love one another and to love God. Religion is the main cause of hatred and war. Humans are the same but different. They may all be of flesh and blood, but their appearances are different, their languages are different, and their cultures are different. But you are all from one source, God. There is no need for division in religion; we just have to love God. It does not have to be in church. God is everywhere. There is no need for a community to share with. You can just speak openly about God to anyone you know. It's ok to love God in your special way. Because you are special, and you all have a unique purpose on this Earth.

The biggest way to heal right now is to be kind and lift your vibration and that of those around you. This will help create a massive, positive shift in all of humanity.

Why does money cause greed?

Money is nothing but a piece of paper or metal. Humans give that paper the highest standard in what they do. What you do in life does not make you who you are. Choose happiness and love. And money will flow to you naturally.

Uplift yourself and others.

What was it like to have Jesus as a son?

He was my son, just like any other mom. He challenged me almost daily, but he was always kind. To be kind to every living thing was part of his journey. Oh, I loved him, and to understand his prophecy was coming when he got older was really difficult for me. I had to pray and trust in my faith because I was about to have my son die for the people to show that God does exist. It was hard for me. Go forth and be kind to others; teach them the way.

Chapter 25

What are we to do to manifest our desires?

Aspirations and goals are great human traits to have. When you find something in your life that gives you meaning and fulfillment, whatever that may be, help an elderly neighbor daily or hold the door for a mother with a small child. These are just some examples of small acts of kindness that people can do daily. They do not go unnoticed. Keep kindness at the forefront of what you do. You will find what fills your desires the most, and then you will know exactly what and how to manifest in your life.

What have you been dreaming of attaining? How do you get it? Being aligned in your true path and focusing on that, everything is a facade on this planet. Nothing is written fully, and you always have free will and can change your fate or path. Sometimes, our thoughts change, but if you focus on your true purpose here on Earth—do no harm to anyone or anything else—you will align with your truest path here faster on Earth.

To attain your dream life by aligning your thoughts to fruition with your path and what you want in this lifetime. Zero in by noting the future as if it is already happening now (because it is happening now, there is no such thing as time or space).

See yourself in the clothes you will be wearing, feel the countertops of your new home, smell the fresh paint on the walls, whatever you desire, and be specific. You make your reality your truth. You can honor your soul's journey by taking more time for yourself to focus on these goals. Go for long walks, get out into nature, rub your feet in the grass, meditate, and cook. Whatever gives you peace and clarity, then write down and journal what you get.

How will people know I am connecting with you, Mary? Will they also understand these aren't just messages for me?

All souls' truths align in a similar way, so your story can be relatable to a stranger. Don't underestimate the power of your being and the reality that you can mold and create. This life is a test to have you accelerate quickly and ascend higher with masters and the Divine on the "other side."

What should we call Heaven? Should we call it the "other side"?

You can call it whatever you wish. We all come from the one true source, God. God has created all, and we can stay as vibrational beings with God when we choose, or we can reincarnate onto planets such as Earth to learn and grow as those vibrational beings. To ascend is to be closer to God, and that is the journey for all souls.

Can souls be destroyed?

No, they can't be destroyed, but they can be recycled in some way. If they choose, they will enter back into God's energy, where they will stay. That is rarer than you think, but it does happen.

How do I know I am connecting with you, Mary?

You see me and feel me everywhere you look. I came to you

when you asked to see a hawk on your walk the other day. You heard the hawk calling out and knew it was a hawk, yet you never physically saw it. That is how I come to you. You have the gift of hearing me (just like anyone who will sit and listen), and I wanted to show you in the same way that you did not need to see the hawk to know that it was a hawk. As you hear me and you don't physically see me, but you know that I am speaking with you, it is indeed me, the Virgin Mary.

Why am I chosen?

I have said to you before that there are many like you. And I kept coming to you every night when you were very tired. We would have very brief chats during which I would explain to you that you are connecting with the Divine. I am so glad you are now sitting and making time to write this book and share beautiful messages that people need to hear. Thank you for being their messenger.

Thank you, Mary.

I want people to keep love at the forefront of what they do because God is love, and if you have God, then all your dreams can be a reality. Trust in me, and I will come to thee. Some dreams are not always in line with your truest path. Then, that dream may not come to fruition. Especially if it is meant to hurt another person, then it definitely won't happen. Keep your heart light, and God will show you the way.

Sometimes, I have trouble with people calling God "he".

Jesus took human form on this Earth, but God has never taken human form. God is in all things and creator but never human. God is neither he nor she, more of everything. The main source of all life, all creation, even beyond the galaxies. What a beautiful and special school that God made for you on Earth. It's just as a mother and a father give your life. They want to see you thrive and be a good person. No one looks at a baby and asks them to grow up to be a criminal. The innocence of a child is something to be cherished. Hold onto the imagination because imagination is not too far off from our true reality, which is otherworldly. Sometimes, in imagination, it holds flashbacks of other places your soul has lived and been.

Dreams can carry these same memories. Understand that you are not crazy, and it is truth and insight into where you are supposed to be in life.

See me in the blade of grass with fresh morning dew.

See me in the grain of sand that will wash up on the shoreline.

See me in a baby's eyes.

See me

See me

See me

Chapter 26

Adam, the alien

Can I really connect with aliens?

Yes.

Yes, you definitely feel different then connecting with God, Spirit, or the Divine. Instead of my usual tingling/vibrating on my head when I am channeling, this feels like a slight humming—almost there, but subtler. Oddly enough, I feel it just over my eyebrows, more specifically my right eyebrow.

That is because we are at different vibrational frequencies than what you have been channeling. We are here to connect with you and answer any questions you may have.

This feels so strange. First, I'm connecting with God, then the Virgin Mary, and now an alien? This is going to be hard for people to understand.

What is to understand? Understanding is to comprehend. There is no comprehension necessary here. There just is. It is not a question of whom you can connect with but where you can connect to. You can connect on many levels. All different dimensions, all different times. This time is relevant to you on Earth, but it is not a concept for us.

Ok, so can you tell me what type of alien you are?

We are what people call the 'Greys' are a gentler species than some, and we do no harm to humans. You asked to connect with an alien who would do you no harm, so here I am.

Would you be able to tell me your name?

There are no words or names to help pronounce it in your language. Let's just say it's Adam.

Ok, Adam, it's nice to meet you.

There is no meet. We have met before, and I come to you often. We have agreed, you and I, to keep a bond between our worlds for science and evolution. I don't do any harm, and it is my job to assist in compliance with the greys to keep you calm.

As I connected with Adam, I could see how he used his hand to wave over my head and calm me. It's almost like he radiates this pulsing wave that sends me off into a deep sleep. He also shows me vividly how his hand looks. His skin looks grey, silky, leathery. He has long arms that fall out to his sides along his thin body and his hands are large with long slender fingers. There are creases, almost like our knuckles along his hand. There is almost a pad shape at the fingertips, which is a little bigger than his knuckle. It feels like he is able to control everything with his

87

mind, and his hand just aides in the direction he wants the energy to go.

I'm baffled. What do I ask you, Adam?

Anything you need. I will answer all the questions.

How long have you been coming to Earth?

We have aided in human evolution for lifetimes. We do not force anything; it is always through agreements and exchanges. We supply the people of Earth with our sophisticated technologies, and in return, we are able to use Earth as a base to hide from other galactic beings.

Not all galactic beings have a like-minded temperament. Some are out to control and conquer. We Greys have always aided and come to people in need.

So, is it actually like Star Wars in the galaxies? That there are intergalactic federations of good and evil?

There are battles across the galaxies of different species of aliens, and some aliens come together to defend or fight to protect one or more species. The Reptilians are the ones who start wars and will fight unjustly. There is no agreement between the Greys and the Reptilians. The Reptilians are out to conquer and destroy other planets and species for their galactic domination. The Reptilians have been seen on spaceships in the Earth's atmosphere. Their ships look like pyramid tripod-shaped ships. They can change direction and fly from any point on the spacecraft.

Inside the spacecraft, there are a couple of chambers. One is for their food and supplies, and another is for their medical use. One area is the cockpit of some sort for operating the spacecraft, and then there is a holding cell for prisoners that they take in.

Usually when this craft is present on Earth there will be sightings of multiple flying UAP's around it. This is us, the Greys or other alien spacecrafts there to defend humans of Earth from these Reptilians.

That all sounds so scary and so ominous. Are we in direct danger?

No. There are more aliens in the galaxy that are out to defend and fight for planet Earth than there are aliens who are looking to destroy it. There will be peace for many years, and there is nothing to worry about now. In a very distant future, humans on Earth will become more light beings and not as humanly formed. There will be a war of worlds where humans will have to help aliens to defend the planet Earth. Much life will be lost, but Earth will be spared and come out victorious.

This is not for many lifetimes, though. Anyone reading this book will not know of this war. There are ways to help protect yourself from harmful aliens. Reptilians do not like water by the bedside. If you keep a glass of water by your bedside when you sleep, they see this as a direct threat because of how water is used on their planet to fight. Water is loaded into high-pressure gun systems. This will definitely prevent them from tampering with you or anyone in your family.

I'm not sure if all of Adam's statements have been accounted for before, but I know I always keep a glass of water by my bedside, and I will surely have one now.

Chapter 27

Good morning Adam, let's get started for today.

I am here for all of your questions.

Where are you right now? Are you on Earth?

I am. I am located off the island of Hawaii in the Pacific Ocean. We stay here discreetly, but I don't want you to know too much about my location because we are always in hiding.

We are constantly moving around and going from galaxy to galaxy. It is our mission to keep Earth in peace and harmony with other galaxies. Earth can be such a delicate planet, and we Greys come to aide humans in creating more environmentally friendly approaches to their world. Don't overuse things, such as food. There is no need for additional waste; it just causes more carbon monoxide in your atmosphere.

The Greys observe this, and we always encourage the people of Earth to do better when it comes to environmental crises. We cannot change Humans to reach this goal, but we do tell them of the harm they are doing to their planet and how to assist in its rebirth.

So, how do we help the Earth and climate change? Is it just as simple as recycling?

There are many ways you can help. Use less. Corporate

businesses push you to buy more, and they make more money. The consumer feels empowered and is given a more euphoric feel when purchases are made. People, especially in the Western hemisphere, buy too many things that they don't need. Life is meant to slow down and enjoy, not get into financial debt because you need the latest and greatest gadget. Stop buying so much, consume less food, and reduce waste.

Waste from Humans is not only with material items but with food waste as well. Buy more foods that are biodegradable and made from the Earth. Compost the little that is uneaten. This is how you can make a huge impact on your climate on planet Earth. Don't be wasteful. Drive less, walk more, or use a bike when you can. All of these things can add up in a big way to help reverse any damages done.

Why do I feel so drained when channeling you, Adam?

I am at a much different frequency, and you are channeling a lot of your energy into my frequency. We are vibrational beings, just as you are. We just vibrate at a much higher frequency.

When you use your mediumship, spirits often connect by lowering their frequency to meet you in the middle.

I don't change my frequency to connect with you; I know how to manipulate your frequency to match mine. This is using more energy than you are used to, and you will feel tired more quickly.

This is also common with alien abductions. After an abduction, a person can feel physically drained. It depends on the species of alien that abducts them and how gentle they are in their process.

Why do abductions happen? Are they necessary? Some people are traumatized by them.

All abductions have different causes. The cause of one abduction may be for facilitating a combined species between humans and aliens. Some are just to assist in reminding humans how they can live a better life. To live in more harmony with nature. It depends on the species of alien, but there is not always one way of interacting. We, Greys, try to make a calm transition so that humans do not get scared when we have them aboard our spaceship, as you call them. Other species are harmful and can leave scratches and even scars.

Most species are just collecting sciences of biology to record any changes in human evolution. This has been centuries of coming and evaluating humans and the changes that they have made from the past until now.

Chapter 28

I am here.

Thank you.

That was me last night in your bedroom, checking on you. Your husband noticed the light too. I have told you that I come to check on you from time to time.

(My husband was awoken last night to a strange light in our room where time ceased to exist because our ceiling fan stopped spinning and stood still in an instant.)

I wasn't scared.

Good, no reason to be. You were once a Grey like us.

I was?

Yes, where do you think your curiosities of space and the moon come into play?

Tell me more of where you come from?

It is a dark planet. No sun near it. This is why instinctively we are created with our big almond shaped eyes with dark, deep layers. We see best in the dark. Now you understand why most alien species are seen at night. We have many powers that are different from humans.

We use our heads for almost any human bodily function. Except where we excrete waste. Our bodies are merely for operating and moving physically in space. To walk, simply said. There is only communication through telekinesis. We are able to project a vast amount of knowledge and pictures to another Grey in seconds flat. They will sense, feel, and know everything we are communicating. For example, I am communicating with you now. But maybe at about 1/10th of the speed to help you grasp the knowledge and write it down manually. It is quite a painstaking process for me to slow down so much.

Well, thank you for that. Otherwise, I am afraid I couldn't keep up.

Oh, you could. You would just have trouble writing and putting it down into words.

We don't process feelings and emotions like humans do.

Space is a vast void, and we know and understand what is. It does not cause us to feel sad or lonely. We just exist, and our true nature is the survival of our species. We are getting smaller in numbers, and this is why we are working to integrate our species with humans. This does not make us sad or upset. It just is. And we work knowingly for a solution.

Humans enjoy the sun. It is too bright for our kind.

That is interesting, and that all makes sense. Thank you, Adam.

Yup.

Chapter 29

Was that you Adam in my room last night? You kind of scared me.

Yes, it was me. I had told you I come to you often.

What were you doing there?

I was protecting you. Unlike some other humans, you have an interest and a pull of energy, which is intriguing to extraterrestrial species. Some want to communicate their demands, but I will not let them. That's when I put you in a deep trance and let you sleep. I mean no harm. I will not harm you or your family.

I am keeping you safe. We greys help humankind and defend the Earth.

Well, thank you. I appreciate the protection. Is there a way to ensure that I don't get scared?

That is not my intention. You had a glass of alcohol, and your body metabolism was not regulating properly, and it can be challenging to manage to keep you in a deep sleep.

Are you the one causing the ringing in my ears? Because I have never had that with spirit?

Yes, I am of a different frequency, and when I try to connect with you, it can sound like ringing in your ears. Like I have said, I can match your frequency, but it is very challenging for me. It is easier for me to bring you up to my frequency.

Are you responsible for other people's well-being on Earth as well?

Many. I don't always have to be physically present to protect. I will send a hologram of sorts to deter any other unwanted invaders.

Unwanted invaders? Like extraterrestrials that mean harm to us?

Exactly. It is a constant battle, and this is my job, and I take pride in it. This is why I have an agreement with the Galactic Alliance to reside on Earth and assist people when they need my help.

When you said you were a Grey alien, I thought that meant you were small.

I didn't say I was small. You assumed so. I have almost humanoid features: two arms, two legs, a torso, and a much larger head. I am about 7 feet tall. There are some of my species that are a bit taller or smaller than me. I have no need for immense strength because my job is not to have physical combat. Not combat between us and humans. Combat between the Greys and other alien species. My intellectual self is much more advanced than anything on Earth. Your new AI is not even comparable.

I lack human emotion because I am not human. I don't process things negatively or positively; it is just to survive and do my job. I will keep you calm.

So, besides protecting me, you have said that you will come to visit me because we have an agreement.

Yes, I will help you advance in your psychic and medium gifts so you can understand Earthly and Universal changes faster. I have made you more sensitive by doing so.

Thank you. Often, when I know that you have visited me, I wake with markings somewhere on my body. During this most recent visit, I had a golf ball-sized bruise on my upper left calf, and on the inside crease of my left leg, there was a circular bruise when I brought my calf up to my thigh. It's definitely sore. Can you explain that?

There is no need to thank; again, this is an agreement you have with the Greys. The marks are sometimes from the transportation process of moving your body in and out of our ship. This specific bruise is for an implant behind your left knee so we can monitor your progress on the upload we just gave you. It'll give us your molecular compounds and help us better understand how fast your download is happening. You seem to be responding to it well.

Do you mean any harm to me by doing that? I have noticed some changes in my psychic activity in the last day. I have been able to pick up on every thought prior to someone saying it, and I am intuitively getting psychic downloads of what a person may be going through.

We will never harm you. This is all for scientific research.

We work with selective people all throughout the world to better understand the evolution of the human race and how you are progressing or regressing.

These people are the more elevated humans who are shifting into the new Earth. We also assist in their transformation. Anyone who is not being upgraded and moving into the enlightened human will be phasing out.

I have been having a lot of activity with you lately but not so much with spirit. Is there a reason for that?

Yes, these changes on Earth are happening more rapidly, and I want you and the people of Earth to understand more about human and alien relationships. We have already discussed that some alien species want to do harm to human beings.

These aliens, who wish humans harm, don't have any agreements with Earth. Their mission is to concur and leave mass destruction in their wake. They are not part of the galactic alliance to keep peace and harmony across the universes.

Your governed officials have been involved in this galactic alliance for many years. Aliens and humans have agreements on how to defend and protect the human race from these hateful species of aliens.

This is why I reside here on Earth as a tall grey: I am constantly defending against attacks from outside aliens. We grey reside in strategic places all over the world to create almost a forcefield on planet Earth. This is to create a barricade from any unwanted invaders coming into Earth's atmosphere.

This sounds a bit scary and like a science fiction film.

Where do you think those ideas come from?

Chapter 30

I was awoken with a noise this morning that is hard to explain. My husband says he has been hearing this noise since you and I have been connecting, maybe about 6 weeks or so.

Yes, that's me.

Can you explain what that noise is?

It's a portal of sorts. Communication in our technology helps us teleport our physical beings from one location in the galaxy to another. We often won't do intergalactic hops and reside somewhere in the galaxy we wish because the transfer will be too fast and too far, which is not far for us to go but to keep our physical beings comfortable. If we teleport out of a galaxy that we are physically in, it can cause us to feel unwell. Not that it's not done, it is. It's just that we prefer to stay within the galaxy we are being transported to.

The best way I can describe the noise is it sounds very organic and electronic at the same time. It sounds almost like water dropping into a bucket, but it has a static radio sound. I heard only one digital sound this morning, which woke me at about 5:30 am. When my husband heard it, he said it will be anywhere in the bedroom, and it can be multiple sounds, like beep, beep. He has also heard it down the hall and at different times throughout the night while we are sleeping.

I was also up a bit last night, connecting with you. I asked you for information on alien technology and things that you have that humans don't so we can better understand technologies that can help advance the human race as well.

While we were discussing that, I saw a ton of files come in telepathically about how aviation works for alien ships, medical treatments, and other things of that nature. But it was all coming in so fast that I don't have a memory of all the paperwork and information coming in. So, how do I retrieve that?

Like I showed you, either through meditation or through hypnosis.

What was everything that you sent me?

It was everything that can help the human race to upgrade technologies and societal hierarchies that we use. It is all information that aides in human intellect and evolution.

Can you tell me exactly what was in those files you sent?

I can send you a re-download 1x1, and we can show the depictions on the following page.

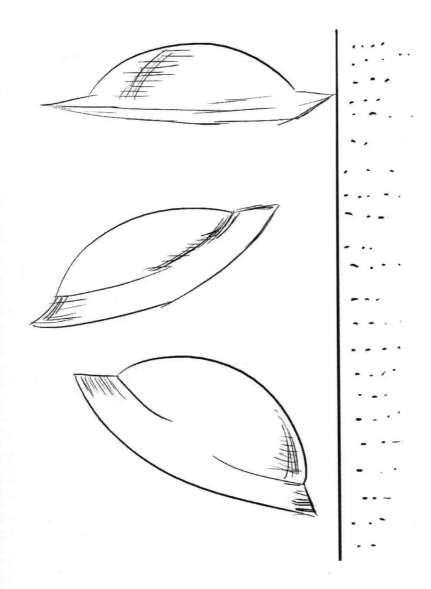

Diagram 1

(My apologies for my rudimentary drawing, but this is similar to one of the images I received.)

Here are our ships. These are our smaller ships where we use for more frequent and fast travel through space and Earth's atmosphere. To the right is our outline of building materials and how to operate the ship.

It just looks like a bunch of dots and lines to me. Can you explain step by step?

To make the structure, there needs to be a zero-gravity space. This is more of the atmospheric pressure we are used to. It allows us to manipulate objects that are much heavier with little to no effort. Once suspended gravity is set into place, one needs to assemble the materials.

The closest natural compound you have on Earth is titanium alloy. Otherwise, there is a naturally produced metal on our planet. The titanium alloy will be strong enough to hold shape but also be light enough to move very rapidly. Like a bullet, for example. And the titanium alloy must be sheet thin. You will need more than 200 sheets for one aircraft.

For Greys, we do not need windows on the craft because we can manipulate vibrational frequencies to move the aircraft and place it in the space and time where we choose to go. We can operate the spacecraft in flight with our thoughts and one simple toggle to have the ship move. Most of our other operating systems are for the use of equipment on board our ships, such as food operating systems or time manipulation.

When we need to process an abduction, we are able to stop time. If it is a busy area and we need to be under little to no human detection, we activate this time stop. As I have said to you before, there is no time in space. We can have people stop in the middle of what they are doing to connect with the humans who are necessary and leave those who are not. If we are seen, it is because we want to be seen.

Us Greys are making sure we are helping with the desensitizing project of humans. This is exactly what we are doing: desensitizing and preparing humans for a more regular and interactive lifestyle with aliens. This is still in the future in quite some ways, but it will be yours and our new reality together. This is also in human evolution and is the reason for the abduction and preparation of your species. We have been working together and will continue to work together more openly.

Our special aircraft are designed to be operated with our signature touch. We have an almost suction-like fingertip that gives us very stable control over the operating system. It's not like a toggle for movement; it's like a small cupped sphere shape. We can put our hand on that shape and manipulate space around our aircraft through a vibrational pull around any atmosphere or space. Only one is needed to operate the smaller ships.

Wow, that all sounds so fascinating. As you are explaining all of this to me, I am thinking of the alien spacecraft that crashed in Roswell, New Mexico, in July of 1947.

I'm wondering why we haven't seen more crashes here on Earth.

As I mentioned, we have complete control of our inflight systems. Very rarely, an error causes us to crash. The cause could have been an inexperienced operator who came into the Earth's atmosphere too quickly and didn't adjust to the difference in pressure and gravity before switching the system to manual. Again, though, crashes are extremely rare.

Some aliens reside here on Earth, and some are merely visiting, all for different purposes and reasons. Again, I am not here to harm any humans in my care. I am here to help them with their physiological and intellectual upgrades.

Chapter 31

This chapter lets us discuss health and wellness. I'm curious about how you, Adam. How do you stay healthy and do you get sick? And how do we as Human beings keep ourselves healthier?

There is no such thing as illness for our species of aliens.

This is not the same for all aliens, but we have evolved so much that any imbalance in our physical beings will be addressed before it even becomes an illness. This is like when Humans get the symptoms starting from a cold; they will often get a sore throat. We don't even get to that stage because our intellect is so powerful that we can see our genetic makeup in our bodies with our minds. And we can make slight alterations on a cellular level to create perfect harmony within our bodies.

We do have healers who are among the Greys as well. This is not for sickness but more so for physical wounds. Our bodies are made up of delicate tissues, like humans. We can bleed and get cuts, lose limbs, and die, and die from forceful trauma. Most wounds can be healed through the Healer using special frequencies. When some cannot be saved, they will die, and their bodies will be recycled into our planet. And then their souls will move to the soul realm where we all reside.

Are you talking about Heaven?

Some humans call the soul realm Heaven. Yes.

So, aliens go to the same place humans go when we die?

Yes. We are all made from Source and return to our birthplace of Source, which is in the soul realm. That is where we decide if we want to reincarnate again or work on lessons to grow and advance our souls.

So, if aliens have souls, why don't you experience feelings like we do? Specifically, love?

We simply observe feelings. We don't process human emotion like you do. It is more of an observation of how we may feel toward someone or something. I suppose there is a sort of love because we can care deeply for each other and our purpose. It is just something that simply is. We don't have anger, greed, fear, or sadness. We, Greys, understand it, but it is not necessary for us to go through the emotion.

I care deeply for our cause—the survival of our species and protecting the humans of planet Earth. I can reflect the emotion of care and love back onto a human. This is where I borrow some of your energy when putting you into a deep slumber. I find the care and devotion inside of you and mask it back to you, amplifying it along with the vibrational frequency to have you in a deep trance-like sleep.

We want to see humanity keep striving and growing. Your evolution directly effects us, so it is vital for us to comply with the alliance and stay focused on our duties to keep Earthly beings safe.

I have heard of a theory that Greys are just evolved humans in the future. They come back in time to assist us in changing our ways to get to our enlightened states.

Humans have been able to travel in time, but it is off in the distant future and is not on a mass scale yet. These sightings are indeed alien species that originate from another galaxy beyond yours.

I want to know your opinion on how humans are to evolve into this state of enlightenment. Some may already be there. How do we get there collectively?

This is all about the human construct of their mindset. When a person is busy at work, in life, or socially, the human brain becomes warped into the three-dimensional world of materials and things necessary for now. Becoming enlightened is to become aware of everything. Everything means your past, present, and your future together. Having knowledge of why things happened instead of asking how things happened?

It's where you become more of an observer of your reality.

You are still able to work and process things, if not more effectively because you can manifest more easily with just a simple thought; when you are more in line with the universe, then you become more in line with yourself.

Some people, few though, have reached an enlightened state on Earth. These are people who have more sensitivities than others. Such as yourself, as a psychic medium. When all are enlightened, they will have this ability as well. To reach enlightenment in the world is going to be the biggest struggle of all. For humans to understand that they are their own worst enemies instead of allies. There is no reason for hate and wars. When peace overcomes your world with absolution, humans will live harmoniously with nature and all the creatures within it. This is where enlightenment will be found for all.

This is where we Greys are helping you all go. The faster this becomes your reality, the faster we all work collectively throughout the universe. This is where all alien species will become more integrated with Human beings on Earth.

Will it be a collaborative and melded society?

In this new Earth, human beings will be able to have their own spaceships readily accessible to all who want to venture into space. It won't take Elon Musk to get you into outer space. It will just be accessible to all. Sort of like your taxis now. Food will be free; there will be no hunger. Similar to us, there will be no need for medicines. When the human mind becomes so evolved, it can heal itself internally at a cellular level, just like we do now.

It will be a sort of utopia where there will be no more hate, no wars. Humans will communicate both telepathically and speaking as they are now, but with fewer words to explain things. It won't be cities that take over, but Humans will live on the lands but not in a nomadic way. More so in a very integrative way. Knowing how to take care of the Earth becomes essential to the survival of the human race, and this is more commonly understood. There will be structures of sorts for council members to hold meetings. But it is woven beautifully into the landscape of Earth, with no harm or pollution emissions from building it or having it up and running.

When I see this building; that Adam is describing to me, it almost looks like the artwork in Chicago, the Bean. You know, the shiny metallic bowed-shaped bean thing in downtown Chicago? How do we make a living on this new Earth or in society?

You will have jobs to tend to, just like now. Instead of jobs that revolve around the corporate world, your new jobs will revolve around your existing world. There will be farmers and markets for goods to be sold. The goods being sold are minimal essentials, nothing excessive like you have now. There will be open kitchens where anyone can be the chef, and anyone can come dine. There is no money necessary for any of these goods or trades because collectively, as a society, there is an understanding that, eventually, you will need to give or trade something in return. It is like an honor system.

This society will have healers who work more energetically to balance your body and well-being. This is because illness is no longer. Your physical body will still be fragile and can get physical wounds. These can be healed by the healers, or if not, the body will return to the Earth in the form of death.

And the process starts all over again.

As you described this, I thought of James Cameron's movie Avatar. They are an enlightened species that live in harmony with nature.

I know about it.

Well, is it like that? What are you describing as our future?

Something like that. Not so blue, though.

Oh, you make jokes now?

No joke, just answering your question.

Ha, well, I found that a little funny. Ok, to ask another question.

I will answer.

Will our new advances in artificial intelligence aide us in

reaching enlightenment in the future or hinder us?

Artificial intelligence will help with certain medical advances and give insight into certain topics that humans can understand.

Overall, the system will be faulty and fail. It is not something that will be used in the fully upgraded society of the New Earth.

I am sorry if we answered this already, but when will this New Earth happen?

It is starting now. It will take years for it to fully form, possibly centuries. The human race is making strides in advancing their intellect and spiritual growth to move towards the enlightened stages.

Centuries? That sounds so long from now.

Within the time of the universe, centuries are not all that far away.

AI is a way for your society to upgrade to another level of technology and learn and grow in the sciences. Humans will learn a lot in this time frame. This step must happen to understand what is truly needed and what is not.

When Humans reach such an enlightened state, they will no longer need AI because they will be more advanced than AI can ever be. This is the ultimate design of Human existence and evolution.

The reasons for waiting for this advancement and taking years are beyond your comprehension. Remember discussing the ripple effect of what one action can lead to another and so on and so on. Well, that is the same with planets, galaxies, and beyond. Just because planet Earth is out here seemingly by itself, which it is not. It is still in direct alignment with the energies of the surrounding planets, and it is directly affected by them and vice versa.

When all this shift happens into the New Earth, there will be no limitations on space travel and collective consciousness. This is the process, and God has made you and will guide you along the way.

So, do you connect with God?

Of course, I do. It is different for me than the way that you do it, though. Humans go to church or pray to feel a connection with God. On the other hand, I will go deep inside myself, and there is God. It is the creator of who I am. So, internally, I will sit and have a meditative space for connecting and hearing God or all consciousness.

There is no need for me to pray. Praying is asking an outside source to help you with your everyday woes or fears. But all you need to do is look within. That's how it is with our species, and there is no need to reach out to anyone for help or guidance. It is done innately and without any judgments or labels. Like I have said before, a lot of what we believe is just is.

He says this almost matter-of-factly and very instinctively.

I always appreciate his direct answers and honesty.

Chapter 32

I wanted to ask you for more of the downloads that you sent me. I haven't been able to access them in my meditations. I will most likely have to have a session with a hypnotherapist. But I have heard of people who have had hypnotherapy before being alien experiencers, and it really frightened them. I don't want to do it if it is going to scare me, but I also want to help advancements in our society and for us to learn from you. So, is this something I need to do to retrieve the information you sent us?

Yes, it is not meant for you to go public with it right away.

You have to be very selective about whom you give this information to. Use your intuition to guide you to the right person. Some government officials would not be in your best interest to share with, but others have just enough say to make a positive change in your world.

You will be in a protective space if you choose to go into hypnotherapy to retrieve this information. It is there and given to you because of your integrity and honesty. You are not corrupted by outside sources, money, or greed. You derive from a place of wanting legitimacy in helping the Human race as a whole. This kindness has not gone unnoticed by you and others. This is where you will advance into being a spiritual leader.

Wow, that feels a little overwhelming. And it makes me feel like I am not worthy.

Oh, but you are. Everyone needs to understand their own self-worth. Everyone needs to hold humility and gratitude in their hearts. If you treat yourself and everyone around you in the way that God sees you, this is absolute love and no remorse or regrets on everything. It all becomes that collective consciousness that will move us all from one being into all beings. Being one with the universe and everything and everyone in it.

At this high elevated consciousness, you will be able to see life within a single blade of grass. This life source comes from the living, breathing planet Earth. It moves through all things grounded to the planet, even inanimate things. Because the energy doesn't stop flowing because a building or a skyscraper is built on the Earth. It connects with the Earth, and it follows flow and energy. It may have a different frequency level, but just because it is inanimate does not mean it doesn't have a frequency of life.

I never thought of buildings having a frequency. But I see it as you are showing me. It's almost like this light that comes from the Earth's core and spreads like fingers or lightning outward. As it reaches the ground level, it continues into anything that touches the ground. I just asked you, well, how does it work for flying objects, like planes? You quickly showed me it is still connected to the light that will carry from the ground through the air outward. That's amazing! Thank you for showing me that.

You are welcome. I am here to help humanity in all ways possible. I am here for any and all questions.

You know, people are going to read this and not understand that I connect with God, the Divine, and now an alien. I have to say sometimes it's a little hard to grasp myself.

What is so hard to believe? If you perceive things like we do, there would be no questioning. Humans are capable of so much more than they are and what they have been told they can be.

Instead of being ridiculed, someone like you should be embraced as a good change in humanity's evolution. No species wants to sit stagnant or go back in time with its evolution. Everyone looks and strives for the next level of consciousness, the next big, new idea that will change things for the better.

Aliens can sit and observe all the on goings on Earth. They can also make slight adjustments to alter the outcome of a human life or human lives collectively. Most aliens are sending messages for humankind to upgrade intellectually and physically. It is through these messengers that people like you are coming into this more heightened awareness and knowing.

Don't be afraid of the changes that are happening to you or around you. Embrace them by accepting your downloads from the universe. Downloads mean the shift in your mindset that doesn't feel like your own. You can get a massive all-knowing of an event or something that may happen in the future. These are your enlightened state coming to fruition and enhancing your psychic awareness.

Some aliens can cause chaos on Earth as well. They almost use the Human race as pawns, as if you are part of their experimental game. This is not who I am- Adam, the Grey you are connecting with. These aliens don't care if harm comes to a human being. They almost think of Humans as the lowest species in all the galaxies. They are sometimes referred to as the chaos creators. If they feel that they don't like something or wish for it to change. They will add destruction or chaos to change the outcome of events taking place in the past, present, or future.

Woah, that doesn't sound very nice. How do we stop them from "messing" with humankind?

When you are more powerful and enlightened beings. These species of aliens will no longer have control over you. Please don't fear; that day is coming much sooner than you think.

Chapter 33

While writing this book, I have discovered so much about myself, my abilities, and the abilities of all humankind. Having conversations with God and the Virgin Mary and now connecting with Adam, the alien, one thing seems to stand out to me the most, and that is love and kindness. Love is the universal language and is understood across the globe.

This book is to help you to expand your personal growth, consciousness, elevate your vibration, and be closer to God. It is to experience life, love, and everything it has to offer. There are always going to be those differences and challenges in our lives. It is how you address them and overcome them quickly without rash action or cause. It is to be more mindful of how you, yes, you, have a huge impact on the universe. How your thoughts and actions affect yourself and others.

Don't be afraid of change. Change can be intimidating or scary, but if it feels right, then it is where you are meant to be. Nothing is permanent, you can always return if it doesn't work out.

I want you to go out and share the experience you received from this book. Pass the torch of light that you may have taken from reading these pages. I am sad to have this book come to an end, but I know it is just the beginning.

ABOUT THE AUTHOR

My journey to becoming a Psychic Medium started in my small town of Florida, New York. It is here that I found my intuitive spirit. After just recently moving to Georgia, I have realized that spirit has been communicating and guiding me on my true path. I feel that being a Psychic Medium is my purpose in life, and I am so excited to get to share my gift with you all!

Made in the USA
Columbia, SC
02 December 2024

48290150R00065